Alongside the child

Experiences in the English primary school

Leonard Marsh

PRAEGER PUBLISHERS
New York · Washington

Books that matter

Published in the United States of America in 1970 by Praeger
Publishers, Inc., 111 Fourth Avenue, New York, N.Y. 10003

Library of Congress Catalog Card Number: 74-114346

Printed in Great Britain

The author and publishers are indebted to John Hunnex for
his photographs of classrooms and children's work.

A note to the reader

Some readers may prefer to read first those chapters which reflect
the everyday classroom situation, postponing chapters two and
four until they have gained a general impression of the book.

Contents

Author's note

I am most grateful to Professor Ben Morris, who, as External Examiner to the Goldsmiths' College, London, Postgraduate Primary Education Department, has been a valuable influence in the development of a pattern of teacher training related to the approach to primary education that I have attempted to outline in this book.

Similarly I owe much to Mr Christian Schiller, who, as External Assessor for teaching practice, has been closely linked with the development of the course. My debt to him extends over the many years during which he has been a constant source of stimulus and guidance.

It gives me great pleasure to acknowledge my indebtedness to Lady Plowden for her inspiration and help. As Chairman of the Goldsmiths' Advanced Primary Course her influence has been deeply appreciated by everyone concerned.

I am indebted to the Warden of the Goldsmiths' College, Dr D. R. Chesterman, for his constant encouragement; to my colleagues Connie Rosen and Dorothy Duncan I offer my gratitude for much friendly discussion and support; to David Gadsby of my publishers, A & C Black, a special note of thanks for his interest in the production of this book. To the members of the Goldsmiths' College one-year part-time advanced course 'The Education of Young Children in the Primary School', and to friends in many schools, and particularly those teaching in Oxfordshire, my thanks for so generously sharing their insights and enthusiasms.

To my own students at Goldsmiths' with their concern for teaching and their continuing contact over the years my thanks for shared experiences. They, and many others too numerous to acknowledge, have contributed richly to the writing of this book.

L. G. M.

Preface

Children go to school to learn. What they learn and how they learn depends upon what we as teachers believe and feel about children. Teachers make the schools what they are. What we know, believe and feel about young children determines our daily actions in school, and it is in the light of this that we should evaluate any discussion of 'the theory of education'. Theory in this sense is vital, for it determines the pattern of practical activity that makes up the working environment of the school.

This book aims to provide discussion material for teachers and students, and to encourage individuals and groups to take a second look at some of the educational theories which they use to guide their work in the primary school. It is not an exhaustive discussion of the whole field, but it gives one or two examples of what is and must remain a continuous evaluation of our actions.

The practical problem which faces primary education is not ignorance. As Christian Schiller writes:

> We are not held back by lack of knowledge. If even half of what is now clearly known were accepted with feeling and carried out with understanding by all the people concerned, the whole picture of our primary schools would change. Of course we have need to know more; but the major problem is to mediate enlightenment regarding what we know already.*

* 'After Plowden' in *Bulletin* of the University of London Institute of Education (summer 1967)

And in this period of dominance by experimental and physical sciences we need to remind ourselves that the basic techniques of the educationalist must be observational, not experimental. We are closer to the biologist than the physicist, and it is the close observational approach of the naturalist that should be our research model in the coming years.

1

Children and their world

This is a book about young children at work in the primary schools. In the best of our junior and infant schools we see children deeply involved in their work and freely using their senses, feelings and intellect to encompass their world. Those who are fortunate enough to spend much of their life with children and teachers in a range of classes and schools know that this pattern of education, with its obvious quality, is rarely found beyond the primary stage.

What are the factors that give a special quality to the learning that takes place in many of our primary schools?

A young child is not at a 'mental distance' from his world:

> A child in full health of his mind will put his hand flat
> on the summer turf, feel it, and give a little shiver of
> private glee at the elastic firmness of the globe. He is
> not thinking how well it will do for some game, or to
> feed the sheep upon . . . he has an ecstatic sense of the
> thing's inherent characteristics.*

The image in the mind, and the actual object, are not clearly differentiated for the young child, and the almost obsessional concern of some adults with reason and intellectualizing is not present in the young child to act as a barrier to the process of feeling deeply and gaining pleasure from sensual experiences. A young child takes an element of *our* world and makes it his own.

* Montague, C. E.

It is this personal relationship, this intermingling of self and experience so that it becomes difficult to differentiate the two, that is a characteristic of the development of understanding in young children. The idea is always shot through with personal sensual experience and it is in this way that a child gets close to the 'inherent characteristics' of things.

This extract from a lengthy piece of writing by ten-year-old Michael reveals the intermingling process:

In grass fields most of the grass is all mixed. I love it like that—not all the same kind. When it is about two feet high and the wind blows over it like a kind of slippery silk, grey more than green and sometimes only the colour of lightness and movement which I suppose you would say isn't any colour at all, it quivers and goes in straight slanting ripples; and even if the wind blows hard it won't hurt it. It only twists the blade. If you break the grass stem at the joint a tube-like pipe is running through it, and if you chew the end it is very hard. If you run your finger up the blade of a cocksfoot grass it cuts your finger, and I should think that's how the word blade for grass originated. If you cut it along the side and suck it, it is very juicy but bitter. Yet I keep doing it. It is silly, I suppose, but I still go on. I expect I shall always go on doing it, even when I am grown-up.

There are all kinds of grasses. The kind called soft meadow has so many hairs on the blade and is so dry the cows don't like it. A meadow full of oat grass looks like sea foam or even detergent, and nearly white too: well, a greeny-white. Cocksfoot has flattened shoots and dull green to real deep *blue* leaves. And that is the truth. And a head of spikelets arranged in one-sided clusters on little wiry branches. Cocksfoot belongs like all the others to the family Graminaceae and its botanical name is Dactylis glomerata.

Oh, we have a wonderful mower. It goes along as
smooth as the wind does, and leaves the grass flat and
straight in rows, and in a line just like the parting in
my dad's hair.

It is, of course, difficult to analyse the quality of learning
which can and does occur in the primary school, but there can be
few teachers who have not become aware of its existence. There
is a world of difference between the situation where the child is
personally involved and that where he is 'going through the
motions' (however helpfully and efficiently) with a task regarded
as 'school learning'. The observer becomes aware of differences
in the set of the shoulders, the placing of the feet, the focusing
of the eyes and countless other details of body posture. One also
becomes aware of the level and rhythm of the conversation, the
intensity, and frequently the duration of concentration revealed.

Teachers daily involved in such situations may wonder at the
nature of the experience that could lead the founder of the
National Association for Gifted Children to say:

Try and rivet the attention of the normal ten-year-old
on any subject for more than ten minutes and I will
guarantee that his mind will have wandered right away
because he has lost interest.

The majority of teachers could provide daily examples of situations that deny the truth of this comment. The most significant
advance in professional competence made by the young teacher is
perhaps in detailed observations within the classroom situation
which are in turn related to the whole pattern of activity in the
classroom. It is unfortunate that much of our educational research begins by isolating elements within the teaching situation
to a point where the whole process becomes almost meaningless.

Through his experience of observing children (who are too
preoccupied with their work to notice they are being observed)

the teacher discovers for himself that children are often deeply absorbed for long periods with objects that adults take for granted. Robin Tanner, discussing the role of the arts through the ages, uses Rilke's phrase, 'to re-enkindle the commonplace' and adds 'to make the trivial memorable'.* This brings into sharp focus the nature of children's responses to their world. In such situations children are deeply absorbed, and we are made aware of the different scale of the world for the young child. Adults returning to childhood haunts often experience a real sense of being ill at ease because—say—a set of church steps thought to be difficult to step up during their childhood is now seen to be quite normal in dimension.

It is the recognition of the vital contribution of the 'inter-mingling process' already discussed and the differences in scale that cause the primary teacher to make the basic working experience not 'The Story of a Bicycle' but, rather, the minutiae of the sensually appreciated environment.

Laurie Lee, remembering his childhood, is nearer the touch-stone for work in the primary school than the numerous and arid accounts of 'Milk' projects:

> I shall never forget that three feet high vision of the world—intimate, down to earth, sharp focus. Like any child I lived at the level of grown-ups' boots, somewhat shorter than summer grass, could look cats and beetles full in the face, knew the knee bones of grasshoppers, the eyes of flies, the mouth of a chewing snail. I could even study the moss on a stone and smell the wings of the bees in the bushes.
>
> It is on the surface of the ground, where most life lives that a child has his natural being. And it is the sharp enjoyment I then experienced—a kind of cheek-

* Tanner, R., 'Creativeness in education', in *Froebel Journal*, no. 5 (June 1966)

by-jowl brotherhood with every insect, vegetable, matchstick and raindrop in the neighbourhood that I recall most vividly today.*

A seven-year-old boy echoing the movements of a piece of paper caught up in a gust of wind blowing across the playground reveals an intensity and spontaneity that involve movement, laughter and an accompanying set of staccato words. His excitement is soon caught by some six or seven other children. The adult onlooker can but marvel at the intensity of the activity and the range of responses involved in such a brief sequence of activity. Similar levels of involvement can be seen in the boy painting in a corner of the classroom, the girl taking a first print from her lino-cut and another writing a poem. We do not always succeed, but it is our purpose in the classroom to make it possible for children to respond to words, paint and other materials as naturally as they do in 'play'.

The problem with various schemes concerned with the reconsideration of 'subjects' or 'forms of knowledge' (interdisciplinary inquiries of the secondary school, projects and the like) or integrated 'studies' is that they fail to take account of the essential and already established personal integration of the young child's life. So many adults are at present concerned with elaborate schemes for integrating a situation that is, from the child's point of view, already integrated! The primary school curriculum recognizes this in that the curriculum has a psychological basis† and it is this understanding of the experience of the child that determines the nature of the teacher's evaluation—rather than a balancing of subject material or establishment of a hierarchical scheme of skills. We do not begin with lists of subjects, but rather with the child's relationship with his world. The specially

* Lee, L. Talk on BBC *Woman's Hour*, 1959
† See *Psychological Foundations of the Curriculum*, W. C. Olson in *Educational Studies and Documents* (Unesco, Paris 1957)

provided school experience uses this fact as a starting-point for the development of situations that will involve meeting items of knowledge, but, more importantly, teaching children how to think rather than what to think. And of course the curriculum includes more than 'how to think', for the activity of the primary school as an institution is concerned with the development of the total personality.

Teachers see in the primary school an extension of the good home. The school environment is planned to influence, to provide opportunities for choice within an appropriate and carefully devised range, and to produce a climate where children experience a mature pattern of social relationships and catch a sense of standard and judgement in this pattern as well as in their work. It is this amalgam of purpose that is the special strength of work in the primary school, and in the chapters that follow there is an attempt to outline and consider in greater detail the professional responsibilities of teachers working with young children.

2

Children learning

The concentration on a narrow range of animal-learning experiments in psychology has meant that the psychological element of our educational theories has tended to underestimate the part played by *imitation* in learning. When one observes learning in any social setting one becomes aware of the vital role of imitation in children learning their world and their place in it.

The imitation goes beyond mere watching and it is because it involves so much of the emotional life of a child that it is so important. The incorporation of experiences through imitation is a process as fundamental as play, and involves the same intermingling of self and observed object. At play the child is at one moment the express engine, of which his sounds and the movement of his hands provide symbolic evidence, and at the next moment he is the engine driver; later he seems to be both engine and driver! It is easy to feel how important the whole process is to the young child and to see how serious he is about it. The child's learning through imitation brings him into a complex social emotional relationship with his learning. (Learning 'through imitation' seems so much more meaningful than the customary 'by imitation'.)

The child's observation is exact. My own three-year-old son once helped to clean the car. Throughout the operation I was aware of a not very helpful intention on his part (not stopped by injunctions about scratching the car or becoming soaked with water!) to do exactly the same as myself. But a clear 'cameo' of observer imitation was revealed in the detail of removing my wellington boots at the kitchen door. David placed his foot at exactly the same angle on the doorstep—merely standing on the doorstep was not enough—and followed the process through as if he were tied to my shadow. Involved in the process, I was hardly aware of the fact that he was watching me, for he seemed so intent on his task; and yet an onlooker was fascinated by the completeness of the imitative process—even down to facial expressions!

Once one considers the part played by imitation, one becomes aware of countless situations that involve parents, neighbours, relations and young children. Mowing the lawn, mending a fuse, mixing cement, repairing toys—these are just a few situations that I can recall from very recent experience with David, aged three. But though the process is easily seen with the pre-school age group (and all students training for teaching should have a programme of observational work with the under-fives), the process goes on through life. I can think of examples with my ten-year-old daughter involved in the domestic routines of the home, while the dressing up and making plays of the nines and tens provides further evidence of the serious and fundamental contribution to a child's learning made by imitation.

Village schools have long worked with family grouping as an educational organization. More recent is the attempt by some larger (and this generally means urban) schools to organize their children in family groupings or mixed-age groups. The large urban infant school (notably in Bristol) has a tradition of family grouping dating back to the mid-1940s, but experiments such as grouping first- and second-year, and third- and fourth-year juniors together, to give a modified grouping, or even in some instances a full spread of the junior years, is a much more recent development. Family grouping needs to be seen not as a contemporary gimmick, or as a fashionable phase; it needs to be evaluated in terms of achieving one's educational aims and solving the problems of practical action.

What is very evident in schools that have adopted family

I

II

grouping is the significance of imitation in the pattern of classroom learning. The ten-year-old spends part of the lunch-time sitting in the rocking-chair and reading to a group of fives, sixes and sevens. The ten-year-old is doing more for herself and her listeners than merely following the pattern set by the teacher. The theory held by the teacher that the primary school is about the process of providing experiences of the 'good family' on a larger scale can be seen in the reality of this lunch-time, and in countless other everyday incidents.

The view of the classroom as a studio, workshop and research area where examples of good craftsmanship (in writing, mathematics and science, as well as the more usual craft activities) are valued, provides a further example of the importance of imitation in learning.

In the case of craft, the process is rather more formal and more easily recognized by the observer. In a situation such as block printing using lino-cuts the teacher deliberately contrives an apprenticeship system in order to pass on skills. An older child making a print has a less experienced inker who works alongside him and thus gains the initial experience. Following comment from the teacher, the 'senior craftsman' and the 'apprentice', working together, both complete prints and then the teacher, acting at this moment as the master craftsman (not unlike the pattern of a Renaissance studio), discusses the work in order to focus on a growth point.

Such a situation has great strength about it in the degree of activation and of social and emotional involvement—much greater than in the formal teacher/class instruction situation, which also depends on an imitative process, debilitated as it is. With such a working situation many of the adult preconceptions about what children can accomplish, and at what stage, are frequently confounded. We just cannot presume to set down such limits for children.

At this point it is sufficient to stress that the vital role in learning played by imitation in the child's pre-school life is widely observed in countless situations. Once one achieves a flexibility of social relationships in the classroom (and though family grouping is not a prerequisite for this, the development of this pattern in some schools can be seen as a highly significant influence) the richness of work situations that follows provides clear observational evidence of the continuing and powerful contribution of imitation to learning in the junior school. It is the writer's view that this factor is significant right through into maturity, but at this stage of growth the term 'influence' is more helpful in the discussion than 'imitation'.

Every teacher is concerned to discover how children learn and we often ask the more limiting question 'How do children think?' The cognitive field of psychological study as a component of any educational theory has been described by Piaget. The study of the development by children of basic concepts and strategies for their thinking involves setting up performance situations (or the time-consuming abstraction of material from normal classroom situations) and the clinical interview technique. Obviously such methods depend to a large extent on our understanding the use of language by the child and the realization that the words spoken by a child do not necessarily reveal the extent or real nature of the child's personal experience (we all know what it is to fumble for words in a despairing effort to express what we feel and know) and cannot pretend to be free from misinterpretation. Despite these difficulties much valuable material has come to hand, and it is the best method we have.

We cannot identify thought with language, but it is clear that language plays a vital part. The use of signs helps us to select and focus on our experience, and provides an essential permanence if we are to range back and forth over an experience in order to develop a sophisticated concept. Language gives the child a greater control over his environment. In order to avoid too didactic and restrictive a view of the role of language it is wise to remember that for the young child (and this should mean throughout the primary school) it nearly always means the mother tongue, and the words used are embedded in the deep personal and emotional relationships of the mother and the family.

Unless there is brain damage, language will help a child to develop a level of concepts that enables him to deal with 'second order' relationships; he will be able to consider past actions and the future as possibilities. With a child suffering from brain injury (due to a difficult birth) whom I had in my class for several years, I noticed that he could 'read' almost faultlessly in a rather mechanical way, but could not answer any questions about the material, other than recite almost verbatim the passage he had just read. In the same way he could perform all the four operations of number quite quickly and correctly. He would add fourteen to eight by finger counting or pencil dots, but could not say whether fourteen was more than eight or less. Language was present, but he was not able to detach the words from the practical concrete situation and thus range back and forth over the experience. But for the normal child language has an important role in fixing the experience in the mind, and enabling the child to detach himself from the immediate concrete situation.

The work of Luria* and Vygotsky† is a fundamental contribution to our knowledge of the development of language and thought, as is the work of Piaget. Once their work is more widely known and the implications acted upon there will not only be a deeper understanding of how children learn, but a sharper vision of the fact that much of the traditional 'English work' is quite inappropriate for the junior school. Bernstein's work on the social determinants of language, with his discussion of the 'restricted code' and the 'elaborated code' of much of our middle-class-based education, serves as a useful reminder to teachers

* Luria, A. R., and Yudovich, F. I., *Speech and the Development of Mental Processes in the Child* (Staples Press 1959)

† Vygotsky, L. S., *Thought and Language* (Wiley, New York, 1962); see also introductory accounts of Russian psychological research in *Educational Psychology in the USSR*, edited by B. and J. Simon (Routledge 1963)

(particularly to those in secondary schools) of the vital inter-action between the child and his family and neighbourhood environment.*

Our discussion of some aspects of language development should serve as a framework for the more detailed discussion of Piaget's investigations into concept development and should remind us of the dangers involved in any piecemeal view of the mother tongue. It should also make clear the implications of this in any investigation that must rely upon 'talking over' the child's experiences with him.

Most readers will be familiar with some of the work of Piaget and it is not intended to describe in great detail any of his many fascinating experiments. Apart from the translated works there are several helpful introductions, by Nathan Isaacs, Brearley and Flavell.† J. McV. Hunt's *Intelligence and Experience*‡ is a valuable book for anyone wanting to discuss the nature of the many psychological theories that make a fruitful contribution to

---

* Bernstein, B., 'A public language: some sociological implications of a linguistic form', in *British Journal of Sociology* 10 (1959); 'Language and social class', in *British Journal of Sociology* 11 (1960); 'Social structure, language and learning', in *Educational Research* 3 (NFER 1961); 'Social class and linguistic development: a theory of social learning', in *Economy Education and Society*, edited by A. H. Halsey, J. Floud, and C. A. Anderson (Free Press of Glencoe, New York, 1961); 'Aspects of language and learning in the genesis of the social process', in *Journal of Child Psychology and Psychiatry* 1 (1961); 'Linguistic codes, hesitation phenomena and intelligence', in *Language and Speech* 5, part 1 (1962); 'Social class, linguistic codes and grammatical elements', in *Language and Speech* 5, part 4 (1962); 'A socio-linguistic approach to social learning', in *Social Science Survey*, edited by J. Gould (Penguin 1965)

† Isaacs, N., articles in *Some Aspects of Piaget's Work* (National Froebel Foundation 1959); Brearley, M., and Hitchfield, E., *A Teacher's Guide to Reading Piaget* (Routledge 1966). More extensive discussion is found in Flavell, J. H., *The Developmental Psychology of Jean Piaget* (Van Nostrand 1963)

‡ Hunt, J. McV., *Intelligence and Experience* (Ronald Press 1964)

our understanding of how children learn. Perhaps, however, we should remind ourselves of some of the details of Piaget's use of the term *stages*. We will do so by specific reference to the development of number. Piaget outlines three main stages of thought:

1. non-operational (birth to two years) or sensory-motor stage;
2. pre-operational stage (two to seven years);
3. (*a*) operational (seven to eleven years) stage of concrete operations,
   (*b*) formal operations (twelve years and over).

The ages given are of course no more than crude groupings, and it is essential to relate any discussion to actual responses to experimental situations. Piaget categorizes the responses as follows: *stage 1* describes those children who cannot answer the questions because they do not understand the principles involved; *stage 2* is a transitional phase, characterized by groping—answers are sometimes correct, sometimes incorrect; *stage 3* is for those who give a correct response and show by their explanations a firm grasp of the concepts involved.

The material obtained from such a developmental approach provides, in its usefulness and closeness to the pattern of work in the junior school, a sharp contrast to that produced by standardized group-attainment tests and survey type testing concentrating on norms.

Piaget outlines a progressive sequence of concept development and it is in the *pre-operational thought* stage (two to four years) that we see the beginnings of symbolic behaviour. Thought is seen in the invention of signs, albeit somewhat rough and ready: 'pussy' stands for rabbits and dogs as well as cats. Naming objects is dominated by the egocentric attitude which causes dolls and favourite engines to be treated as living things. It is one thing actually to carry out an action and quite another and more difficult thing to reproduce actions in thought. It is this process that is, in a technical sense, an operation.

In the *intuitive thought* period (four to seven years) there is an absence of conservation and an inability to reverse operations. The classic experiment with the counting of beads into two glass jars illustrates the point well. The experimenter counts beads into a jar and watches the young child's actions in doing the same. When the process is complete children at this stage have no difficulty in agreeing that each jar contains the same number of beads, but once one jar of beads is emptied into a taller thinner jar children think that the quantity has changed. In passing it should be mentioned that the writer has found it by no means unusual to find a few children still at this stage (for some of these experiments) in their first year in the junior school. Obviously the child's thinking is dominated by the perceptual features of a particular situation: he is too involved with present action to be able to relate the two factors.

With some children the situation, if distorted to extremes, does reveal the beginnings of the ability to reverse the operation and once this is achieved as a consistent and deliberate pattern one has the period of *concrete operations* (seven to eleven years). At this stage the child has a set of strategies or systems, is no longer tied to particular states of objects, and is able to co-ordinate separate viewpoints into a system that triumphs over perceptual instabilities and gives an equilibrium to the child's ideas. The teacher uses this Piagetian development analysis to evaluate, for example, the emergence of a concept of number.

The concepts of space and time are formed at this stage and though the operations are not logical the fact that the child has mastered them in concrete situations represents a major step forward in the growth of intelligence. The child's actions are now given a logical coherent structure, even if this does not at this stage extend to verbal propositions or 'thought activities'.

In the *intuitive phase* (five to seven years) children think that if two plasticine balls have changed shape their size, weight and volume have changed as well, and though in the period of concrete operations (seven to eleven years) children appreciate the conservation of weight as well as that of substance, they cannot see conservation of volume. They are able to recognize the operation of two variables, that what an object gains in length it loses in thickness, but they cannot apply the third variable.

The *concrete operations* stage shows a varying pattern of development according to the particular practical situation and application; the operations are still tied to items of concrete experience and it is not until the stage of *formal operations* (eleven to fourteen years) that various operations are interrelated on the basis of formal logical principles.

It is clear that the analysis of children's thinking outlined by Piaget gives the teacher a psychological theory of the utmost significance in its influence on the practical provision of learning situations in the junior school, and for the evaluation of children's responses to situations.

The implications of the theory have been worked out most clearly in relation to mathematical and scientific experience, but it is clear that there are similar consequences for other fields of experience. The work of Goldman* is but a beginning of what will be a very difficult reappraisal of the role of religious education.

The purpose of this chapter so far has been to remind readers of the kind of contribution we can expect psychological material to make to our theory of education. The discussion has been restricted to two major fields of inquiry that have, quite clearly, had a major influence on how teachers view the learning situation in the classroom. The full implications have yet to be worked out in practice and much has yet to be done. Though the discussion has been restricted to two major fields of inquiry, we must add that there is still much in what we frequently refer to as *Gestalt psychology* that remains to be actively considered by teachers.

Gestalt psychology in the sense of a separate school of psychology had its beginnings in 1912. It was in reaction to the earlier

---

* Goldman, R. J., *Religious Thinking from Childhood to Adolescence* (Routledge 1964)

stimulus-response-dominated psychology of Thorndike and others, and in opposition to the behaviourist theories of Watson and others. By the 1940s these competing schools of psychology could be said to have become merged into a unified body of psychological study characteristic of the adolescent period of the development of the subject rather than its early childhood.

It is well known that Gestalt psychology made its strongest contribution in the field of perception. The stress on good organization of perceptual material, the need for the learner to make his own 'closures' in learning, and the importance of whole structures and patterns still repays close study today. The stress on the total field theory for the growth of intellectual powers is in close accord with the work patterns developed in our primary schools and supports the general statements made about the learning situation and process by most writers about the primary school.

Many teachers have an intuitive understanding of Gestalt principles of psychology. They see the growth of intellectual powers in terms of well-organized concrete situations, and in relation to the continuous interaction between child and environment, and they realize the importance of social expectations to learning. Much of the practical work of the classroom would gain greater intellectual acceptance, and, perhaps, greater precision in practice, if the elements of the Gestalt contribution to psychological theories were more firmly and widely known by teachers. For example, the earlier stimulus-response theories were still dominant in the teaching of mathematics until the 1950s despite the Gestalt experimental work that had long been available. Indeed, it is only very recently that such a book as Wertheimer's *Productive Thinking** has had any real impact on the discussion of problem solving in mathematics.

Piaget's objection to Gestalt psychological theories is that there is always a danger of replacing the verbalism of the earlier formal

---

* Wertheimer, M., *Productive Thinking* (now published by Tavistock Publications 1966)

methods with a 'verbalism of the image'; that is, remaining on the level of figural thinking instead of progressing to operational thinking. The intuitive perceptually based learning outlined in Gestalt psychology was an improvement on the verbal learning of the earlier period and elements of the approach are still valuable. However, the 'active' view of knowledge outlined by Piaget, that knowledge is not the contemplation in one's mind of copies of things, but rather a result of the individual's actions on the object and of the process of internalization of these actions into thought, provides the most satisfactory guide for the teacher. The account of Piaget's lecture on 'Children's Thinking—the Figural Aspect and the Operational Aspect' is an illuminating account of this central problem.*

Much of the discussion of ideas about learning in this chapter is, perhaps, intuitively perceived by many teachers. It is certainly true that the ideas outlined are very much in accordance with the work patterns of many primary schools and that in a general sense they lend support to the developing pattern of primary education.

* Some books providing a framework for the further study of learning processes:
Ellis, W. D. (ed.), *A Source Book of Gestalt Psychology* (Harcourt Brace, New York, 1938)
Flavell, J. H., *The Developmental Psychology of Jean Piaget* (Van Nostrand, New York, 1963)
Hebb, D. O., *The Organisation of Behaviour* (Wiley, New York, 1961)
Hunt, J. McV., *Intelligence and Experience* (Ronald Press 1964)
McKellar, P., *A Textbook of Human Psychology* (Cohen 1952); *Imagination and Thinking* (Cohen 1957)
Thomson, R., *The Psychology of Thinking* (Penguin 1959)
Vygotsky, L. S., *Thought and Language* (Wiley, New York, 1962)
Wertheimer, M., *Productive Thinking* (Tavistock Publications 1966)

3

Painting and talking

We rightly regard the primary school as an autonomous institution within the education system. It is clear that it has realized its potential most fully when it has discounted any consideration of its curriculum in terms of preparation for any subsequent stage of education. Historically the creative ethos that now runs through the whole pattern of activity of the modern primary school was first revealed in the field of art and craft—particularly in children's painting.

It was due to the revolutionary views of Professor Cizec, who saw that children's paintings had their own artistic validity, that the children's personal experience was first considered as the focus for the curriculum of the primary school. With the work of Marion Richardson* we saw the beginning of the process that was to produce the creative ethos that now guides the whole pattern of activity in the primary school.

It was in painting that the problems of freedom and guidance, the fundamental importance of sensual experience and the nature of the complex process of expression, were first met by teachers. The implications of sensual experience for the education of young children were first understood by teachers who had become used to observing their children deeply absorbed with their painting.

* Marion Richardson began her work as an Inspector under the old London County Council and she spread the use of large sheets of paper, large brushes, and powder paints and encouraged free and independent painting by children.

A. L. Stone* in his account of the development of his school in Birmingham describes the order of the development of the curriculum in his school and comments: 'It seems to me to be wrong to teach academic subjects *before* children have experience of expression in the arts.' Certainly it seems clear from my own observations that, whether with teachers in training or in the development of a creative ethos in a primary school, the beginnings of the process are seen to be in the activities of painting, sketching, and modelling with clay; this beginning period is protracted, and care must be taken to ensure that these activities can progress and be intermingled with other activities, no matter what the stage of development of individual or school.

Obviously we are suggesting that experience of the arts is a vital preliminary. It is important that teachers should be aware why such activities provide such a fundamental ground for the curriculum of the primary school.

In any discussion of the place of painting, modelling with clay and the use of other media it seems important to start from the experience of young children. It is the writer's view that the 'ground experience' is a dynamic sensuous one which is to some extent intermingled in apparently highly abstract mental activities such as mathematics. Those adults engaged in intellectual abstractions are often unable, or unwilling, to think over their primitive sensuous experiences which provided the ground for their abstractions. Stravinsky's description of his own process of composition in which he has the image of piano keys being depressed as he is involved in writing the musical notation symbols is a particularly stimulating account of the process.

When observing young children we see them using their bodies as the first medium for expression. 'Jumping for joy' is the lay observer's recognition of the process and 'movement' in the sense

---

* *Story of a School* (HMSO 1949). The only personal account of a school ever published by the then Ministry of Education

discussed by teachers drawing on the work of Laban* is clearly a basic and powerful form of expression and appears first in the developmental sequence. Though not discussed, the importance of the reciprocal effect of movement upon the emotional state is recognized. Young children respond to many situations through movement and this is the beginning of creative work in the primary school. Using the mother tongue follows this, and then the use of paint, clay and other materials as mediums for expression.

Today many schools are very much concerned with what they term 'creative writing' and this activity has become the centre-piece of their work. Many teachers who have not been involved in the development of a general creative ethos for their school have begun to show interest in techniques for the development of creative writing. They see in the techniques discussed a way of improving the quality of one of 'the three Rs' and it is this more limited intention that is the cause of much of the enthusiasm for children's writing.

The account of 'creative writing' by Sheila Lane† reveals that children can write 'better' if their writing comes from activity and experience, but the account does not make clear that, if we are to ensure that such writing does not in time lose the distinctive quality of children's creative activity, then the writing must be seen as a thread of the children's experience rather than becoming a major preoccupation of teachers.

Writing is a difficult medium and we need to recognize that it is a relatively late development for children in the primary school.

* Laban, R., and Lawrence, F. C., *Effort* (Macdonald and Evans 1947)
† Lane, S. M., and Kemp, M., *An Approach to Creative Writing in the Primary School* (Blackie 1967). Earlier discussions of this topic can be found in Langdon, M., *Let the Children Write* (Longmans 1961); Pym, D., *Free Writing* (University of Bristol Institute of Education— University of London Press 1956). Clegg, A. B., *The Excitement of Writing* (Chatto 1964) is an anthology of writing that represents a more widely based classroom experience, and thus preserves the essential ethos of the primary school.

Much of the writing that at present takes place in the primary school is talk, recorded in ink merely because there is no one to listen to the talk or because the teachers' anxiety is such that they feel the child 'must write something'. The more plentiful supply of tape-recorders should change the balance.

So often the concern of the child is not with communication as such, but the personal need to relive his own experience. Certainly the idea of writing *because* it enables one to communicate with someone removed both in space and time does not occur to the young child. When he writes: 'I went into the sea and got my pants and woolly all wet' or 'I went to the rock pool and cut my toe, it stings very much', he is concerned with coming to terms with the original experience rather than trying to communicate with a person removed from him by time and space. It happens to appear as written marks on paper, but its real nature is talk.

The teacher in the primary school has to try to ensure that the contemporary overconcentration on 'writing' is not such that the primacy of the relationship between experience and expression through the mother tongue is overburdened by the too difficult forms of expression. Much that is now written should not in fact be taken out of the context of experience and talk, which the child has developed together.

Writing as a medium has a purpose outside the child's experience. This means that writing as a creative medium is too pure or abstract to be the most appropriate expression for the majority of primary school children before their third year in the junior section. The wholeness or oneness of the child and his experience needs to be kept constantly in mind if the creative response is to flourish.

It is because of this complexity, and the fact that the appreciation of the situation removed both in space and time comes much later to children than many have assumed, that the organization of primary education in terms of 'Junior Mixed and Infant' is so important. Such an organization permits a continuity of care and a more ready acceptance of children where they are, because there is no need to be anxious about 'preparing for the new school'. Fewer assumptions are made about targets at the age of seven, and assumptions are not used as criteria for curriculum planning.*

Richardson's account† of his work in New Zealand and Stone's account‡ of his school in Birmingham illustrate the importance of the arts in education and are evidence of the order of development that has already been described—both for individuals and schools. Painting is an early medium of expression, as is clay. Later comes the growing power with the mother tongue, and this quality of absorption is extended into writing (seen with the 'rising tens') in the case of individuals, and for schools when considerable progress is made towards personal choice by the child and the untimetabled day pattern of working.

Since the 1930s increasing numbers of teachers have discovered through their own classroom experience that children can paint with confidence and enjoyment. The free bold use of paint produces paintings that have the distinctive quality of a child's creativity. As we gain more experience in accepting the dynamic quality of sensuous experience and its importance as a ground experience throughout the curriculum, so we are beginning to see the distinctive quality of children's creativity with such activities as mathematical abstraction. The teacher in the primary school accepts that feelings and facts are intermingled and that he must get alongside the personal experience of the individual. Of course, there is no evidence within the practice of the primary school to suggest that teachers attempt to confine the idea of creativity to the arts, and indeed discovery approaches imply a creative view of the whole curriculum. It is misleading to discuss such terms as

* Marsh, L. G., 'Plowden: some implications for the training of teachers' in *Bulletin* of the University of London Institute of Education (summer 1967)

† Richardson, E., *In the Early World* (New Zealand Council for Educational Research 1964)

‡ *Story of a School* (HMSO 1949)

creative unless the context indicates that we are not using the word in the literal sense.

Much of the discussion of the term creativity depends upon an understanding of the rhythm and harmony in the pattern of social relationships within the modern primary classroom. This situation requires the use of a chain of words such as studio, workshop, reference area* if we are to begin to hold in the mind the complexity of the classroom.

With a physical arrangement of bays and 'corners' (see chapter 11 for a fuller discussion of this topic) we have the development of a co-operative working relationship where the teacher works within an 'untimetabled day' programme† in order to concentrate on the enrichment and elaboration of experience. To the child's experience of one example of the colour brown the teacher brings experiences of browns from many situations and many materials. Much of the work done will be individual, but small groups and even more often pairs of children will frequently work together. It is with this background in mind that one goes on to explore further the kinds of experience involved in painting and other media.

It is unfortunate that some recent writers on primary education have isolated their discussion of such terms as 'creativity' from the general pattern of teacher and children's activity within the classroom. This has led them to give considerable attention to the discussion of such obviously inadequate and crude models of the teacher's role as one who allows 'self-expression' or 'uncorks the bottle so that emotional tensions can be relieved'. Such casual and superficial discussions of the teacher's role in relation to the development of children's painting neglects the extension of sensitivity involved in any drawing or painting based on careful

---

* See 'Development projects, Junior School, Amersham', in *Building Bulletin*, no. 16 (HMSO 1958), for an introductory description of this point.

† See chapters 11 and 12 for a fuller discussion

and absorbing observation of natural materials. Such a use of the
environment is a characteristic activity of the primary school, and
forms part of the total experience that is expressed in the act of
painting.

Young children respond to direct contact with paint and clay.
They touch the paint, they spread the paint with their fingers and
generally explore the materials. But this enjoyment of the exploration of the material itself seems also to carry with it a desire
to make something.

A four-year-old seemingly puts three blobs of paint on paper,
but asks you to 'come and see my big fierce jungle bird'. Children
paint and use their paintings as symbols for something they have
thought about. Sometimes it will be a painting of 'the big red bus'
and on another occasion it will be 'my mother'. Because of the
emotional content of the subject of such a picture one *may*
see emotions being clarified and defined through the act of
painting.

Most teachers are familiar with the 'family pictures' that contain large mothers with much detail and small shadowy fathers
almost out of the picture! Much of the painting at this stage
requires careful control and selection of materials (including the
provision of clean water), the arrangement of conditions in which
the child feels secure, and a time span that allows the child to
become absorbed in the process of expressing his experience.
Time to talk, to listen, to ponder and to reflect is part of the
painting process in the classroom.

Fairy tales, ships and the sea, houses, monsters, animals and
woods are themes frequently chosen by children and explored
in the early stages of the primary school. Painting of this kind is
an important means of expression for a child's fantasy life. Later
the everyday environment of the child (remembering that the
child is not a mere onlooker in his environment) begins to take
over from the fantasy environment and he will want to shape
much of this everyday experience through his paintings. Painting
and clay modelling is the child's most important language in

III

IV

V

handling symbols for nightmares, parents, fears and loves, and the unknown world of witches and dragons, and such expression serves a vital function for the individual.

Paintings of cats, dogs, a shell or piece of bark frequently reveal close observation. When the child has chosen the object himself we often see in the painting the child's attempt to convey to others something of his personal experience of the situation. The painting is not just a cat but a very special and personal cat. 'It's the neighbour's cat that always comes to me after it's had a fight.' As with the use of the mother tongue as a means of expression, we see in such paintings the reality of the experience, the shaping of experience that involves countless day-to-day encounters if feelings and attitudes are to be ordered and appreciated. Just as children talk over the steps they are taking, so in a painting they experiment and work out potential meanings.

Sometimes the painting (and the talk) requires an audience, but often the other person is really redundant and it becomes, as with five-year-old David, a conversation within oneself. The sequence of talk reveals how young children use talk to help them organize their experience, to select items of that experience for special attention and to try out possibilities in their minds. This flexible, confident, wide-ranging expression (and it is this) can be used by teachers in schools, in the same way that we now use painting, as a major activity of the school day. The recorded sequence of David's play reproduced below lasted some twenty-five minutes. It was not selected from a large number of recordings, but was a random period of solitary play with model cars and building bricks. The sequence has not been edited for significant passages or modified in any respect.

DAVID. Making a garage here—there's petrol pumps of course.
Um um um here's where [*pause*] this should go on.
This should go on here and that's a sign . . . and, those are petrol
   pumps and that's a key. That's the people at the bus stop.

Um um I think I need those bricks over there. It's easy to knock down.

I am not going to make that, I think.

Um that's for cars [*arranges bricks as platforms on towers*] that's for cars to go on.

Um this is the lift up thing.

It's taking two at the time. [*He means the platforms already built for cars.*]

It is that lift truck.

There it takes two at a time. Um er and now I am going to build up um where they store their things and I am just going to get

And there's one. That's one of the ends and now here on the other roof

I am going to get some more bricks.

This is going up there—the brick on top of it

Very wobbly this might be, um whoops

I know, two of these. This is er is what's-a-name it's a — for things for cars to go on as well [*almost singing*].

And where's the other one and underneath, actually, is a post.

If it falls it won't fall on the ground—that's a mattress so the cars won't scratch.

I can fit another one on there.

Ah! that will better.

This is a plank, it will go better on a plank.

Now some more cars to put on there.

And I got another one.

This will be signs for old cars.

And they are going to

they haven't got brakes and that sort of thing [*pause*].

What cars shall I put on there?

I think I will put a police car.

Police cars.

That will go on there [*pause*].

I am going to put that up there.

It looks a bit untidy.

I am going to use these things.
If some fall on I am going to put some on top.
I am going to use these things.
If some fall on . . . I am going to put some on top.
They are models.
And here is only for one car.
And only for one car.
This one is for one car.
One very small car model.
These are at the back.
And they are going to look at them—while they make them in the factory.
That, this is the factory.
They will start near the factory.
They have to have signs of what they are going to make.
And um um I think, I put
We've got the petrol pumps here. [*At this stage David looks over the various constructions and arrangements of cars.*]
What else? Cars? House? I can't do that.
I think I could make a wobbly line.
Cash office? I haven't got a cash . . . No!
Office, office. I will make some signs.
Some small signs people too.
I work on this garage and that's what the sign says.
I can't read it.
Um um um [*pause*].
A building and a roof.
Cars in the window. I can't make a car.
What else?

A factory of cars um um um
Pretend this is the garage factory.
I will tidy up this bit and I will do another bit [*pause*].
I will put that there—on each end that will, that will stick up to a little pole and, and,

I am getting the pole ready.

Doesn't always stand up. If it doesn't that end end won't be used. That will that will stick up to a little pole and and if it doesn't that end won't be used. It needs something stronger.

I know, that's easy to put up.

Put them on, right up there.

That on there, that on there and there's the other side.

The signs, the signs, where's the other signs.

I don't know where the other signs I had um um um [*The ums develop into a singing, humming-like pattern.*]

And here's a green round thing, turns all the things round.

This is a standing up place.

Here is some ladders. If I can get the ladders.

If . . . putting up for window cleaners.

And the houses.

Here's one window cleaner.

Here's two houses. [*He places two number ladders against the side of the bed that is in the corner of the room.*]

That's the river on the other side.

That's the road on that side.

I think—road don't—pass this sign.

Where the fall of water

And a sign. That's what it does say.

I've got—that looks like a real garage over there.

The house, it's a bit away from there.

That's just the factory and petrol pump.

That's been left to be taken off with the cars.

I can't make it stand up.

All white.

That's what it says.

And that's And that's um um [*humming*].

And that's a round pole and that's a what's-'is-name pole.

A garage had a round. Not in the garage in the street it says 'No
  Parking'.
We haven't got another stick-up sign.

Plastic, it's very nice.
We could make a pond with it. It's a private pond.
It's got water supply. It's in the water supply bit, where they—
  where, if I had glue I could stick it together. Glue.
I put it there. That's the water supply bit.
I can't make it stay. The water goes along into there—back in the
  curved bit.
Turns it—into—it makes petrol—from that water.
When it rains it does more good—to petrol.
I known people don't like rain. [*Lengthy pause.*]
I do.
It gives a bit of a clean and scrub.
You don't need to wash then.
Looks a bit tidy now.
That car fell down—put it up again.
It doesn't fall on the mattress.
That one's the dangerous one.
That one; it will fall. It hasn't got a mattress underneath.
That one isn't dangerous. [*He moves the blocks.*] Make it stand up,
  like I usually did. A level one on this high one. [*There follows
  an extended period of building with blocks without talk.*]
The car doesn't actually stand on it.
I think this one I am going to put up high.
This one on a big high one—if I can make it stand up.

It's a whole car, it's easy to make.
Where's the sign. The sign's not easy to put on.

Extra car lifter. It can't be used that's the aeroplane bit.
I can make it go there. Everything I want I've got.

It's not easy to make them stand [*fixing aeroplane on top of a raised flat brick*]. They are, I had better stand up for a minute, just have my rest. Then I—Here's the thing to stop the robbers from stealing some of the models.

That's the bullet bit.

I am going to make a real model now.

That's the cutter and this little bit holds them on.

And I [*hums*]

I am

It had two things, that car on that bit.

I am going to put the garage cars now.

One petrol, both petrol lorries.

And they are all the same signs.

They are all the same signs, so you are all going to one place.

I know,

they put the cars round the side of the garage. This is where they ['*singing*' *noises*].

This is where they go, fit this one [*moves a car*] in.

If it sunk it could easily be rescued by aeroplane.

As it goes on water and lifts the boat up if it really sinks. The hooks hold up the boat.

And where's the men it goes down, flying and then hooks it on as easy as that.

A few more cars in the garage in the outside window. This racing car. When I've done this I will — the train.

There are special ones [*points to a set of vintage cars*] just going to be delivered to people's houses. So they are ready in the background outside.

Where are the scissors

scissors   scissors   scissors

sciss . . . sciss . . . sciss . . . sciss . . . it's easy to cut out.

With this extract of a young child talking while playing with model cars and building bricks we see how important the mother tongue is to the child. The almost continuous monologue echoes the activity; it makes conscious, for the child, the process of selection and of abstraction, so that the experience can be assimilated. In order to do this he quite plainly does not require an audience.

Of course, as the child moves into the primary school and, more particularly, into the last two years of the junior section, the talk leads more readily into writing and a conscious consideration of an audience. But at the earlier stages it is the experience that is held in the mind and the talk is directed towards the exploration of this experience in order to deepen the personal grasp of the situation. It is this use of talk, corresponding to the use of painting and modelling, which now needs more encouragement and stress within many primary schools.

Talk, like paint, is an easy medium for children who are involved in the exploration of their experience, and if we are concerned with the quality of their experience we must encourage as a means of gaining deeper experiences the use of the medium in which they are most able. In talk children can shape their experiences, bring order to their day-to-day encounters in the environment and to their feelings and attitudes. The self-initiated task brings in its train a web of talk and in relation to this activity the child's peers and his teacher try to highlight new elements and new connections for him.

This highlighting process depends upon talk and it is at this point that it is vital for the teacher to come alongside the child, his language and his experience. The intermingling process* is also seen in the relationship between experience and expression in painting.

With the older children in the primary school painting frequently involves close observation of the minutiae of the environment.

---

* Already discussed (page 24) in relation to the experience provided and the mother tongue and the importance of talk (because it is a medium specially suited to the age group)

This is a part of the process of heightening sensual awareness in the child. Sensation and thought intermingle and form the basis for the further exploration and recognition of pattern in the environment. Though much of the painting will be 'as the child imagines it to be', previous visual experience will be a clear influence on the painting and the observation will be the stimulus for the extension of techniques. Print making, using blocks of wood, a range of objects in their own right or fixed to a base to form a pattern, and texture rubbings, will from time to time be used as an element within a painting, as well as in their own right. Experiments will be made with various paints, dyes and inks. The range of media will be extended to include modelling not only with clay but with wood and, less frequently, stone as well.

By providing only a limited range of materials, and by carefully selecting items for display, the teacher can encourage the child's ability to use paint well. The teacher arranges an exhibition of, say, browns, using an interesting collection of items of natural materials. Children in the class then become involved in the further collection of examples of browns. Though some of the items brought in may be crude plastic items with little subtlety of colour, the initial display made by the teacher will generally ensure that children become sensitive to seeking out the normally unnoticed examples. With this background of objects children will then explore the colour brown through observation and then attempting to 'make the brown' which matches. There will be a richer pattern of associations to bring to the painting and a deeper experience of what we can mean when we say 'brown'. During this whole process the teacher's comments and selection will ensure that children gain the experience of mixing powder colour in a rich way so that their colours reflect their increased understanding of the appropriate almost oil-like use of powder colour.

The close observation of the display of browns leads into attempts to make copies of the original colours, using sections of an object to suggest patterns and using this experience to lead into freer pattern-making and, of course, a more powerful command of the media throughout the range of painting activities.

The influence of the teacher is not seen in the setting of the subject (hardly a task requiring the professional expertise of a teacher) or the introduction of 'colour-mixing charts', but rather in pulling the child back to the original experience and causing him to deepen his original appreciation.

The child's autonomy is preserved throughout the process; he has personal control, for example, over the selection of items from the display and the arrangement of these in a pattern that will form the guide lines for his own abstraction into pattern or picture. Alongside this personal response the teacher has the legitimate influence of selection and highlighting of materials, extension of media available and, of course, a share in the discussion of ideas and techniques.* The interaction of the teacher and the child in this situation gives the child a developing sense of power and extends his ability to use painting as a means of expression. In this way, the teacher does not do harm to 'the expression' nor does he become a helpless bystander at the free unfolding of latent psychological symbols requiring the attention of the psycho-analyst.

The concentration on the small-scale environment at the primary stage means that for much of his work the child will naturally turn to painting, sketching and modelling as a means of expression. In the early days he will make simple records of textures in his environment with wax rubbings of bark, brick, iron and countless other surfaces around the school. These collections will be enough for the young child and the rubbings will be displayed in their own right. But later the appreciation of texture gained will be used for other purposes. 'That special tombstone in the churchyard will be just right for the rubbing I shall need for the cover of my book on churches' is typical of the remarks that reveal a growing power of forethought and appropriate selection on the part of the child.

* See chapter 11 for further discussion of this point

The experience of seeking out textures will mean that many paintings will be a mixture of techniques and one may see, for example, a carefully observed and subtle drawing of a shell that uses coloured pencils, inks and paints and is drawn on a background that has been made by rubbing a candle over the paper to get a texture rubbing of a lobster-pot and then bringing out the pattern by the application of Brusho-dye. The solution found by the child is not always a pure one in terms of technique, but it is frequently very successful. Printing, using the end-grain of various blocks of wood and all the vegetables (even including marrow) can first be done for its own sake and then to make patterns of all kinds, with the addition of further techniques such as resist methods, printing-out a pattern on cloth dyed with permanganate of potash by the use of a bleach such as lemon juice on the printing surface of a cut potato.*

The work that begins with seeking out interesting textures within the environment and develops into a range of print-making activities has a twofold effect. It encourages children to look more closely at their environment and to bring to their classroom situation a richer and deeper sensuous experience. It also brings them into contact with the discipline experienced by the craftsman responding to his materials. Print-making requires careful mixing of dyes and inks; the block must be carefully placed and the total pattern thought out. To succeed requires an appreciation of many factors and the pace of work is *necessarily* slow. There is an absorption and a reflective quality encouraged by a wide range of art and craft situations, and this pattern of activity will set the pattern for all the work of the primary school.

The teacher will, of course, encourage this work, not only by the provision of a wider range of materials but also and more significantly by allowing the necessary extended working time

* The Dryad publications on art and craft are a source of useful techniques. Details from Dryad Press, Northgates, Leicester.

more freely than would be acceptable in the traditional subject-orientated primary school.

Thus art and craft experiences in the primary school have a fourfold claim to primacy: (a) power of expression in the media develops early, and children can easily use painting, drawing and modelling to express much of their investigation within the environment; (b) the symbolism the child is able to achieve in his paintings is such that he can come to terms with much of his basic psychological experience; (c) the use of a wide range of media can bring the child back to his environment, causing him to look more closely and to know more deeply through his own personal experience; (d) the time scale implicit in responding to the discipline of materials such as paint, dyes and clay develops a working pattern that underpins the total pattern of work within the primary school.

The exploration of a particular colour, for example, is a basic theme approach that is extended into many craft situations and, in turn, to a wider field of interest for many children within a class. The interest in dyeing leads into the investigation of various ways of making natural dyes; the collection of wool with all the processes through to spinning and weaving. The colour photograph XX shows a piece of cloth made from wool gathered from the hedgerows, carded and spun by primary school children, and coloured by them with natural dyes.

In many areas this will be linked with the study of the wool trade and thus, in this example, the typically wide-ranging consequences of a well-chosen practical activity and its contribution to the curriculum of a primary school is seen. Unfortunately the wide-ranging nature of such work and its important consequences for the organization of the classroom work in terms of space and time sequences receives little or no attention in the contemporary concern for curriculum renewal or change.

The serious disadvantages in considering the curriculum of the primary school from the point of view of 'mathematics', 'science' or some similar classification are clearly seen in any discussion of the importance of the nature of the basic experience offered to children and the discussion of their developing powers of expression. One can easily imagine the consequences of some semi-official curriculum research team being set up within the field of art and craft, the usual limited and hasty discussion of criteria for the subject (generally related to what a specialist requires of the study), the countless handbooks and guide-books, the sample projects and the introduction of a new range of materials would set at risk the gradual evolution of the creative ethos for this work within the primary school. Such an approach would neglect what has been the theme of this discussion of 'painting and talking'— that there is a special relationship between what children experience with their senses and the media of expression we call 'painting' and 'talking'.

4

Developing a learning theory in mathematics

We are in the midst of very obvious changes in the teaching of mathematics. The pressure from our technologically orientated society, together with the much-publicized demands for more and better qualified scientists and technicians, is such that most teachers feel the need to make some changes in their approach. The need for change has long been recognized. The beginnings of a more satisfactory pattern were noticed by some observers before the war, and the 1950s saw a great deal of worthwhile experiment and progress. However, the pressures today are of a different order and there is an urgent need for teachers to set out an effective educational theory to guide the process of change in the next decade, otherwise we shall expend much energy to speed the departure of the human machine of the Bob Cratchit era only to replace it with the equal tyranny of a technologically dominated computation-based curriculum.

Failure to clarify our theory will mean that the present concern with mathematics will not have a significant or long-term effect on schools, and that the contemporary scene will appear, in retrospect, to be a gimmick-ridden period of shallow curriculum reform. Much of the present pressure for change is merely concerned with changes in content, whereas the fundamental need is for an evaluation of the nature of the learning pattern appropriate for young children.

Any theoretical framework that is to play a significant part in determining educational practice (and many of the present theories are quite pointless in view of their complete inability to produce any practical action) must take account of historical, psychological and, in part, of sociological factors. Mathematics is important to the curriculum of the junior school because it is part of our cultural heritage, and because this form of knowledge gives children a sense of control and power over their world that can be interesting and exciting. There never was an *educational* theory for producing through our system of elementary education a race of Bob Cratchits, and there cannot today be a theory which has a similar view, albeit disguised by the intervention of the computer and base-two computation in the school. Curriculum planning that takes a technological view of mathematics as the reason for change must result in an inadequate analysis.

First we must relate our discussion of a development of an appropriate theory of learning mathematics to the 'teaching climate' as well as the influences of our contemporary society.

There is in teaching quite a well-known phenomenon that one meets in almost any school and I sometimes refer to it as the 'Will Hay effect'. Those who still have some hopes for the English film industry will remember some of the many bad films and the few good films that featured Will Hay. If you have not shown Will Hay's *Oh Mr Porter* to upper juniors, hurry to do so before the library copy finally disintegrates! There are many subtle sequences worthy of study, but the overall effect for the teacher watching this film with upper juniors is one of physical pain as the children are at first submerged and then fully involved in the incredible and intense laughter that always accompanies this film.

But for my 'Will Hay effect' I must direct your attention to another of Will Hay's films. The scene is the battlefield in Flanders more than a decade after the end of the 1914–18 War. A party of tourists are quite overcome by the vastness and stillness of this flat battlefield stretching away to the far distance. One of them notices what seems to be a puff of smoke in this completely stilled non-living area and the sharp contrast draws the party towards it. As they get nearer they see that it is a mound and that the mound is increasing in size. Once at the mound they realize it is, in fact, a pile of empty corned-beef tins and, as one of the party mounts the pile to peer down the other side, Will Hay, from his position in the shell-hole, looks up over his rimless spectacles and says, 'Is it over?'

There is, obviously, a delayed time scale in communication, and nowhere is it more noticeable than in politics and education. When we talk of change in education (revolution, fortunately, is never an appropriate term) it is as well to remind ourselves of the Will Hay effect! There is usually a delay of some two decades (it is often more) between the work of the pioneers and the filtering downwards of experimental work.

The process of change is the most fascinating element of any study in education, and one of the better reasons for setting up schools and bothering to train teachers is that in schools one can provide a climate in which change is possible. Christian Schiller has an apt description of the process of change—he likens it to the progress of a worm.

> When I was a small boy in a Victorian home I used to hear my elders talk about 'Progress'. I didn't know what it meant, and I wasn't interested. But I learnt later that 'Progress' meant the way things change. They believed that we were all engaged in a stately procession through the years moving ever onwards and upwards to a desirable destination which was happy and glorious.
>
> By the time I was a young man it was clear that the stately procession had broken down; and with my friends I thought much as students think today: that a big bang would be the best way to bring improvement.
>
> Now, looking back over fifty years of working life, I have grave doubt if there ever was a stately procession, and I am deeply grateful that in this country people do

not like bangs of any kind. It is certain there has been change.

Our schools and what the children do and become in them are quite different from those of fifty or even twenty years ago. But the movement of this change is difficult to detect and describe. To me it resembles nothing so much as the movement of a worm, an earth worm.

An earth worm lies placid on the ground. Its head rises and begins to tug and tug and tug forward, while the rest of the worm remains completely undisturbed. Then another small part of the worm, perhaps called the neck, joins the head in its persistent tug, while the rest of the worm remains completely undisturbed. The tugging becomes stronger and stronger, a tiny ripple forms along the top of the worm and begins to travel further and further along the body. The worm becomes restless, and finally as the ripple reaches the tail it heaves its body forward to join the head. Again the worm lies placid on the ground, until the whole process starts again.

The movement of change is not a steady advance on an even front; nor is it a series of charges after brilliant ideas. The major force in the movement is the patient and persistent pulling of pioneers, scattered far and wide, each at work in his or her school, determined to find a way in which their children shall live and learn more abundantly.

Of course there have been great men and women whose vision and action have inspired a generation: Robert Owen, Friedrich Froebel, in our own time Margaret

VI

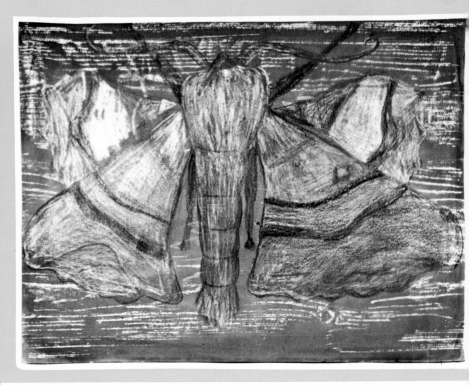

Macmillan, and others. But they pass away, and their ideas pass with them unless these ideas are fashioned into new forms which reflect new circumstances and stand the test of new practices in the contemporary scene. The pioneers take such ideas and refashion and temper them in their daily work in school. Patiently, day after day, week after week and year after year they make the pathway from the past through the present towards the future. Courageous, lonely, and unrecorded, it is from these pioneers that we inherit the present forms of our problems.

The metaphor has changed. It is pleasanter to think of a pioneer than of a worm. But the movement in each image is the same: the movement is on the ground because it is on the ground that change in our schools takes place.*

It would be difficult to give a more accurate description of the process of large-scale educational change and we should do well to accept the implications of this in our planning.

There is also a question of the general climate that determines the type of questions that are likely to be asked—the answers given are likely to be less significant in revealing the climate! An obvious example can be taken from the contribution of psychological forms of thought to our recent educational theories about abilities and the organizational consequences seen in streaming, etc. At the zenith of the psychometric influence the questions asked were concerned with ways of improving tests and their reliability. Few questioned the process of testing in relation to our assumptions about the nature of human ability (constancy of scores and the nature of the environmental influences). As far as teachers are concerned the climate in mathematics was—and this

* Christian Schiller in a letter to the author, later published in *Froebel Bulletin*

is the personal childhood experience of the majority of our present teaching force—characterized by Ballard's statement:

> There is, I fear, no help for it. We must face the cold fact that arithmetic, however much it is doctored or dressed up, is not an interesting subject to the ordinary young child.*

One's response to this statement may well reveal a crude theory of learning.

Theory one holds that arithmetic is an uninteresting and even unpleasant subject, but we must try to get the interest of the children (we are not 'against' pleasure learning), so let's make the subject more palatable by linking it to sweets and apples: 3 apples + 3 apples equals 6 apples, or worse still 3 sweets + 4 apples equals 7!

In *theory two*, on the other hand, we must exercise the human faculties. Let us provide 'mental training' and 'discipline'—the more Latin and Greek and mathematics the better, for it will produce 'trained minds'. This, presumably, implies a belief that the 'trained mind' nurtured on Latin and Greek will transfer its habits of logical thought to all other subjects—rather like learning poetry in order to improve the memory for the names of the various English wild flowers!

Educational theory demands a recognition of the complexity of the field and the ramifications involving the contributory disciplines. Our rather light-hearted discussion of general influences within the teaching 'climate' sets the scene for brief reference to the historical development of the teaching of mathematics. Without the perspective that comes from considering the historical development there is a real danger that the present changes will be superficial, and in this event mathematics will once more be

---

* Ballard, P. B., *Teaching the Essentials of Arithmetic* (University of London Press 1928)

isolated from the basic working pattern of the primary school.

The first research into the subject was by the Americans in the second decade of this century and this led to a restriction of the type of examples included in textbooks. The American surveys emphasized that the mathematics required for normal social situations was not much more than addition, subtraction, some multiplication and the giving of change. Allied to the restrictions derived from surveys of social usage was the view of the nature of mathematics learning based on theories of Thorndike and the American learning theorists.* Thorndike's stimulus-response theory of learning dominated the teaching of mathematics to young children from 1910 to 1950.

In this country Ballard† was a major influence and his hierarchical view of a series of separate items to be organized in a series of learning habits produced the characteristic pattern of an 'arithmetic lesson' in the junior school. Schonell‡ added an increased emphasis on individual diagnosis of difficulties and did much to prevent a return to excessively computation-based work. However, it remained impossible to bring the subject into line with the general patterns of learning developing in other fields of experience in the junior school, and it was not until the 1950s that a major reappraisal took place.

The period 1949–60 deserves a detailed analysis, but for the purposes of this brief historical survey it is sufficient to mention three elements. The first of these was the work of Catherine Stern,§ who sought to build up a pattern of mathematical learning based on principles other than stimulus-response learning; in connection with this the influence of Gestalt psychology on the

* Thorndike, E. L., *Educational Psychology* and *The Psychology of Arithmetic* (Macmillan, New York, 1922)

† Ballard, P. B., *Teaching the Essentials of Arithmetic* (University of London Press 1928)

‡ Schonell, F. J., *Diagnosis of Individual Difficulties in Arithmetic* (Oliver and Boyd 1937)

§ Stern, C., *Children Discover Arithmetic* (Harrap 1953)

teaching of reading and the general emphasis on 'field methods' has been significant. These theories are still capable of extension in relation to the learning of mathematics. The second factor of special importance in influencing the development of a new climate in a large number of schools was the publication of the Mathematical Association's Report *The Teaching of Mathematics in the Primary School* in 1956. The successor to the report is now eagerly awaited. The third factor was, of course, the contribution of Piaget to our knowledge of the way children think.

It is to the work of Piaget, Bruner and the more general psychological discussion advanced by J. McV. Hunt, D. O. Hebb and others* that we need to look for the development of an adequate educational theory for our work in mathematics in the junior school.

First Piaget developed a method of study that provided a vital and urgently needed counterbalance to the psychometric testing (National Foundation for Educational Research, Vernon, Wiseman and others). The method was well summarized by Claparède:

> The clinical method, therefore, which is also an art, the art of questioning, does not confine itself to superficial observations, but aims at capturing what is hidden behind the immediate appearance of things. It analyses down to its ultimate constituents the least little remark

---

* Piaget, J., *The Psychology of Intelligence* (Routledge 1950); *The Child's Conception of Number* (Routledge 1952); *The Child's Conception of Geometry* (Routledge 1960); Bruner, J. S., 'The act of discovery', in *Harvard Educational Review*, no. 31 (1961); 'Learning about learning', *Cooperative Research Monograph*, no. 15 (Government Printing Office, Washington, 1966); Bruner, J. S., Olver, R. R., and Greenfield, P. M., *Studies in Cognitive Growth* (Wiley, New York, 1966); Hunt, J. M., *Intelligence and Experience* (Ronald Press 1964); Hebb, D. O., *The Organisation of Behaviour* (Wiley, New York, 1949)

made by the young subjects. It does not give up the
struggle when the child gives incomprehensible or con-
tradictory answers, but only follows closer in chase of
the ever-receding thought, drives it from cover, pursues
and tracks it down till it can seize it, dissect it and lay
bare the secret of its composition.*

Susan Isaacs voiced doubts about Piaget's early experimental
work. She questioned how far the kind of 'ego-centric' behaviour
described by Piaget was specific to his experimental situations
and how far it extended to the everyday learning of the child in
the classroom and outside. She suggested that the difference between adults and children is not that the former do not reason or
that they only reason in the form of perceptual judgement or
practical manipulation, but that the children's reasoning, which
is essentially based on their personal problems, has less need for
clear verbal formulation.

Piaget provides a developmental theory which explains a
child's growth in mathematical ideas (indeed, his intellectual
growth) in terms of the child's own action and the process of
internalization of these actions. Piaget's emphasis on investigating
the processes of thought has produced experimental evidence for
a pattern of mathematical learning that formerly had to depend
for its justification on rather more generalized statements about
'ways of learning in the primary school'.

It is important that we remind ourselves that the Piagetian
analysis of development gives us a profile for any individual
which will show various stages of concept level at any given time.
The stage of development for number will be different from that
for weight or volume, and there is never any justification for an
umbrella statement such as 'concrete operations' level or 'formal
operations'.

* In the introduction to Piaget, J., *The Language and Thought of the
Child* (Kegan Paul 1926)

Accounts of junior school curricula have traditionally been concerned with the larger 'total field' learning situation, and the contribution of the Gestalt school* was much more in accordance with the development of the primary school than was the work of the behaviourists (for example, Thorndike, Pavlov and, more recently, Skinner). The work of Catherine Stern† is interesting for its examples of the application of such Gestalt 'laws' as 'closure' and 'good organization' to the 'four rules of number'. Indeed, there is much within this period of development of psychological theories that is of value today, though it is the more recent work of Piaget, Inhelder, Bruner and Luria that has brought a sharper intellectual scrutiny and power to the psychological theories contributing to a theory of primary education. An encouraging aspect of this work has been the support gained for much of the practice of the primary school that has been developed largely as a result of intuitive and sensitive teachers observing children and acting on their observations.

Piaget's experimental work has underlined the importance of the early play experiences of young children. There are elements of this exploratory play experience that are seen to be vital to later periods of mathematical and scientific explorations, and it is possible to derive psychological support (see Dienes, Z. P., *Building Up Mathematics*)‡ for the practice of teachers who for many years have arranged discovery situations so as to encourage this kind of pattern and rhythm in learning. Piaget's work reveals clearly that the child is the agent of his own learning and that learning takes place as a result of continuous interaction between the child and his environment. The junior school emphasis on concrete situations is paralleled by Piaget's analysis of the stages

---

* See Katz, D., *Gestalt Psychology* (Methuen 1951); and Wertheimer, M., *Productive Thinking* (Tavistock Publications 1966) for accounts of Gestalt psychology

† Stern, C., *Children Discover Arithmetic* (Harrap 1953)

‡ Dienes, Z. P., *Building Up Mathematics* (Hutchinson, rev. ed., 1960)

in development of thought, and his discussion of the *process* of learning in terms of *assimilation* and *accommodations* provides a learning theory that is an essential element in any educational theory for the primary school concerned with the guiding of a pattern of learning by discovery.

The teacher working in the light of these experimental findings in the field of, say, mathematics sees the importance of individual differences and the impossibility of thinking in terms of classes of children or chronological ages, but at the same time he is able to act against a general background knowledge of the developmental sequences that all children pass through. Though we cannot determine the exact developmental stage of a child, we can accept Piaget's stage of 'concrete operations' as very roughly matching the period of the junior school. Moreover, the view that intellectual activity involves the internalization of actions means that the teacher can devise an appropriate action situation through the provision of materials. The materials permit the child to become his own agent of learning with the teacher in a counsellor-guide role.

In classic Piagetian conservation situations children show their natural reaching out for experience and the seriousness with which they tackle situations. The four-year-old whose thought processes are governed by global perceptions (if it looks more, it is more) will be convinced that a short wide jar of liquid when poured into a tall thin jar *is* more. He is making sense of his world, but he is not ready for situations that depend for their successful solution on a firm experience of conservation. But some six-year-olds will show, in their desire for continued experiment and uncertain discussion, that they are near the time when, in many situations but not all, their concepts will regulate their impressions.

The ordinary classroom situation in the primary school provides countless examples of children involved in experimental and performance situations not unlike the more formal experiments devised by Piaget. These everyday working situations give powerful support for the view that the process of solving problems is a complex activity that is not adequately nurtured by a linear programme of work.

The work of Piaget has underlined the complexity of the development of concepts and his work has been a significant influence in recent years. But for the teacher in the primary school Piaget's experimental focus on concept development is not enough. The teacher's vital professional concern is with the problem of helping children to explore the world of being and process abstraction. Abstraction is of special concern to the mathematician, but the level of abstraction must be kept appropriate and reasonable for children.

The nature of this problem is discussed by Christian Schiller:

> Young children explore the world of existence and soon find themselves in situations in which many different feelings and facts are 'grown together' like the tangled fibres of a root. Bit by bit they learn to focus attention on a particular fibre, to distinguish it, to draw it out, or *abstract* it and learn more about this fibre. They find they are able to deal better with the situation, the 'grown together' or concrete situation, as a whole. Sometimes the problem presented by the situation can be solved only by abstracting one element and dealing with this abstracted from the situation as a whole—this occurs in mathematics.
>
> Abstraction is a process: the fibre can be drawn from the root a little way, a long way, or altogether. In the nature of the study of mathematics the abstraction is complete.*

Thinking is a complex activity the teacher needs to recognize;

* Letter to the author

that he must not sift out this complexity for his children, if they are to learn in a way that is meaningful and useful to them. The process of discovery does not reflect the neat pattern in the mind of the adult who has trodden the path before, and there is no advantage in imposing this foreknowledge on the children. The groping stage is essential if a child is to make an idea his own. The hierarchical topic system of elementary mathematics outlined by Ballard* and others, and exemplified in the practice of schools from 1930 to 1950, cuts children off from the possibility of personal choice and responsibility within their own intellectual activity.

The teacher's concern to help children explore mathematical ideas in the modern primary school has resulted in the reduction of the influence of the 'conditioning' type of learning, which involved activities based on a linear programme, and a new emphasis on what are termed 'discovery approaches'. In a fundamental way primary schools are concerned with an education which matures the personal autonomy of the child. Each individual must feel responsible for shaping his own experience and understanding. Of course, the educational process required for this is a subtle and complex one and if the child is to exercise choice it is clear that the teacher has an overall responsibility for the gradation of experience and related choice. The modern primary school, with its discovery approaches derived from the personal experience of teachers, is now in the position of seeing its long-established practice become the enthusiastic concern of those psychologists (Jerome Bruner is an example) who are involved in breaking away from the classical theories of motivation and the theories of learning association, now represented by Skinner and his work. The majority of contemporary curriculum projects have based their programmes on rather loosely described discovery approaches, and it is unfortunate that they have not

* Ballard, P. B., *Teaching the Essentials of Arithmetic* (University of London Press 1928)

used some of their resources to undertake experimental studies of the 'discovery approach' within selected classrooms. That would have provided an enriching strand to the teacher's understanding of the classroom situation.

Discovery approaches within the primary school are based on the hypothesis that the acceptance of children's relationship with their work and current interests provides a serious starting-point for classroom activity. Discovery approaches help to overcome one of the major difficulties in the teaching of mathematics (and, of course, other fields of knowledge), which is that the child cannot match the teacher's use of language to his own experiences. In the discovery situation the children are not trying to come to terms with the language structure of the teacher (who knows what he is going to say, and is thus always at a different point in the logical exposition than is the listener); they are taking part in the formation of the idea, jointly sifting out alternatives and ranging back and forth over the material in order to set up their own patterns of thought. There is a difference between the situation where you are merely involved in 'learning about it' and that where you are 'discovering something'.

The differences most clearly revealed in the classroom situation are those stemming from personal control or autonomy: the attempt to find pattern, regularity (asking the question 'Will it always work?') with the range of constructive strategies employed; and the increased time span associated with the learning—the ranging over associated ideas and generally more complex patterning of the activity. It is this type of 'discovery learning' that makes for the special quality of learning associated with the best of our primary schools.

The teacher concerned with the development of understanding is primarily concerned with the process of abstraction revealed by children. Clearly the teacher is concerned with ensuring that children have the experience of exploring the world of existence in order that they may have the opportunity to develop their ability to draw out or abstract mathematical ideas.

In this connection I am indebted to Christian Schiller for drawing my attention to the following statement by Bertrand Russell:

> Thoughts and feelings, minds and physical objects *exist*. But universals do not exist in this sense: we shall say that they *subsist* or *have being*, where 'being' is opposed to 'existence' as being timeless. The world of universals, therefore, may also be described as the world of being. The world of being is unchangeable, rigid, exact, delightful to the mathematician . . . and all who love perfection more than life. The world of existence is fleeting, vague, without sharp boundaries, without any clear plan or arrangement, but it contains all thoughts and feelings, all the data of sense, and all physical objects, everything that can do either good and harm, everything that makes any difference to the value of life and the world. According to our temperaments, we shall prefer the contemplation of the one or of the other . . . But the truth is that both have the same claim on our impartial attention, both are real.*

We now recognize the need for experience. No one can make sense of mathematical symbols unless he has carried out actions with materials. Mathematical symbols refer to activities and a study of the development of ideas reveals that man learnt by physical experience and then went on to symbolize his understanding. The four rules of number were, originally, manual operations carried out on an abacus. The mathematical idea does not, of course, reside in the materials but in the abstraction of the actions undertaken with the materials. The actions can be very simple—for example, moving the finger up a number ladder or bringing two sets of counters together; both actions contain the idea of addition. The discovery approach enables the child to

* Russell, B., *The Problems of Philosophy* (Oxford University Press 1967)

use symbols to describe his *own* manipulations of material.*

The importance of actions with objects is soon revealed in the dialogue of a small group of children involved in (for example) the manipulation of Stern-type blocks and a hundred track. P. Ya Galperin† makes the point that:

> The child cannot learn a new action by means of a single observation 'purely theoretically'; he first becomes familiar with a new action in the course of activity with external things—he learns to count, add and subtract with objects. Thus an action that must, in due course, become a mental action is not originally formed as such, but as an external and material action.

Galperin further suggests that:

> It would be incorrect, therefore, to attribute the advantages of activity with external objects only to its visual graphic nature. Such activity is significant, not because it illustrates a mental action but because the child discovers the objective, concrete content of the action for himself, and achieves his first practical mastery of the content.

Jennifer, Rosemary, Paul and Alec (aged seven-plus) were in their second term in the junior school and spent some time in each week working as a small group with various types of mathematical apparatus. With their class teacher they had learnt some of their multiplication tables, though in the context of a traditional pencil and paper formal textbook class teaching situation. In this

---

* Marsh, L. G., *Children Explore Mathematics* (A & C Black 1964), chapter 2, for examples of approaches used by teachers to avoid the confusion that comes from a gap between the approach adopted by the teacher and the level of abstraction achieved by the child

† Galperin, P. Ya., in *Educational Psychology in the USSR* edited by B. and J. Simon (Routledge 1963)

sense they 'knew their two times table', but their response to the performance situation with the number track and Stern blocks indicated the limited nature of their experience.

They had filled the number track with matched colour pairs of units (two greens, two yellows and so on) and Rosemary and Alec agreed that they had made their 'five times' on the number track, while Paul and Jennifer confirmed that there were a hundred ones in the track. I then asked:

OBSERVER. So how many twos do you think we have in the hundred track?

PAUL. Ten.

ALEC. No.

ROSEMARY. No.

PAUL. Ten tens.

OBSERVER [*pointing to the alternating colour pattern and touching several of the twos*]. How many of these twos do you think we have in the hundred track?

PAUL. Ten.

ALEC. Oh! This is going to be hard.

Various suggestions were made. 'We could do it with tens.' 'We could do the tens by just putting them on top and then count the tens on twos.'

The sequence is reported more fully in *Approach to Mathematics*,* but this brief extract indicates how far away the children were from any refined strategy. Dottrens underlines the need for personal experience:

> In order to 'save time' some schools do away with the stage of 'groping' and deprive the child of an essential step in the process of assimilation and understanding; it is quicker to say and to make the child learn that 'four

* Marsh, L. G., *Approach to Mathematics* (A & C Black 1970) threes make twelve' than to permit a child to struggle with the elements which will enable him to find out for himself.*

Children working with materials reveal that time and time again they return to 'simple' experiences as a preliminary to extending their scheme for tackling a problem. The process of problem solving has a rhythm and pattern, but is far more complex than any linear model suggested by studies of animal learning. The protracted sifting and groping period is revealed in the following record of the group's exploration of eights and its development into an investigation of odd and even numbers.† The group (Jennifer, Rosemary, Alec and Paul) filled the number track with eight-blocks. After a discussion sequence concerned with the number of eights in the number track, the group began to consider odd and even numbers.

ALEC. Eight is an even number because you can split it up.

PAUL. So if you gave four children one each it would be even.

ALEC. Ah yes, that would be easy, but if you had two and split that up you would have two fours so you'd give that four to one boy and that four to another.

ROSEMARY. 'I see eight as an even number and we have filled up the track with eights. Will the eight always come out an even number?'

ALEC AND PAUL. No, not always. No.

PAUL. It comes to an even number when it comes to eight, but after that I am not certain.

[*later, investigating 24.*]

ROSEMARY. Yes, because two you can split up and four you can

* Dottrens, R., *The Primary School Curriculum* (UNESCO Monograph on Education 1962)

† See Marsh, L. G., *Approach to Mathematics* (A & C Black 1970), chapter 8, for a further account

split up. Next one is thirty-two. Two you can split up, but three you can't.

JENNIFER. It'll be one left over.

PAUL. Alec! Alec! It doesn't matter which way it makes an odd number. If you wanted to split them up [32] you would have to have thirty-two children. They all have one each.

ALEC. Ah! Ah! but it isn't an odd number.

PAUL. It's an odd number because you can put one there and one there and that wouldn't have one.

[*He arranges three 'ten' blocks and two units as shown.*]

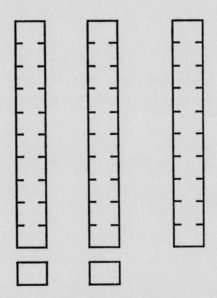

ROSEMARY. Two boys will have eleven each but the last boy would only have ten, so that isn't an even number.

PAUL. No, that's an odd one.

Thirty-two was clearly too large a number for the group to maintain their rather uncertain idea of 'sharing by two', which was in turn intermingled with the idea of 'sharing' and even numbers being 'fair', but when the observer drew out a group of four blocks, Paul immediately said:

PAUL. Two boys can have two each.
ALEC. *I* was trying to do that with thirty-two.
PAUL. You can do that in the same way.

The observational records of the group activity underline the need for children to be in control of their own strategies, to have the opportunity to range back and forth over their experience and to pull out (or abstract) from the complex situation the mathematical idea (odd and even numbers in the sequence above). Children must be given time to focus on the finer elements of the situation if they are to see through the problem. This kind of activity allows children to rearrange their experience, use their language in a social context to extend their understanding and finally to use symbols to record their discoveries.

It is with the process of abstraction that the teacher plans discovery situations for children. The provision of materials shifts the balance from following instructional material provided externally to performance situations that enable children to bring into correspondence their language and the operation. The sifting out of the particular action (the abstraction process) develops the concept of 'fiveness', or the idea of addition, multiplication, subtraction and division. The personal autonomy that comes from such performance situations results in substantial active involvement and responsibility for a high level of problem-solving activity.

> The all-important principle of insightful and dynamic learning is that the concepts and resulting techniques should arise as natural consequences of children's experiences; once we have made sure of this point, other details are less important.*

* Dienes, Z. P., *Building Up Mathematics* (Hutchinson, rev. ed., 1960)

IX

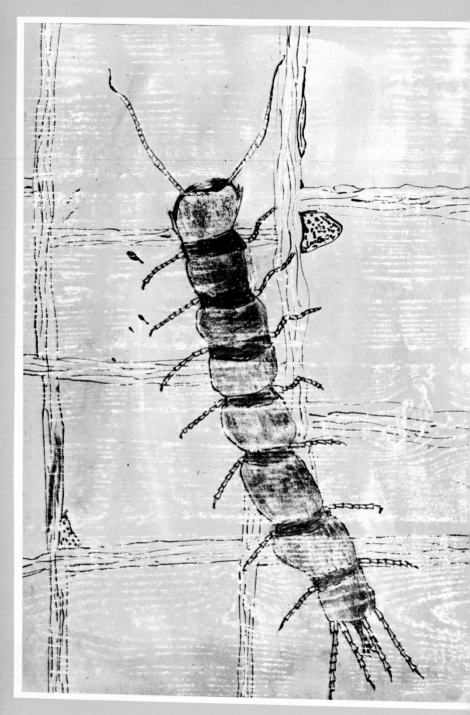

X

'Making sure of this point' has been the concern of many teachers for the last decade or more and as a result we now have evidence of a classroom pattern of mathematical activity that enables children to explore mathematical ideas with confidence and excitement. Indeed, we have now reached the stage where the work in mathematics provides the opportunities for personal choice, involvement and understanding, long associated with the work of children involved in painting.

5

Discovery approaches in the primary school

There is a richness associated with the work of children in primary schools that has no parallel at any other stage of our educational system. Because teachers now confidently accept the challenge of both stimulating and guiding personal discovery work within, say, the field of painting, it is perhaps easy to forget that this pattern of work is of comparatively recent origin. In the late 1930s many teachers refused to believe that it was possible for young children to paint with the freshness and originality that everyone now takes for granted. Now teachers who do not think of themselves as artists have learned not to impose spurious adult standards nor to leave children to flounder.

The even more recent development of the sensitive use of the minute details of our environment (bark, grasses, shells and rocks are examples) to stimulate close observation of texture and colour provide further evidence of the qualities and richness of young children's work; and in the last decade there has been a remarkable flowering in the personal writing now undertaken by children in the primary school.*

Teachers who are not specialists are happy to encourage children into a pattern of open-ended experiences which involves choice and which demands the full use of the child's emotional and intellectual powers. But for some teachers this approach has

---

* Clegg, A. B., *The Excitement of Writing* (Chatto 1964); and the *Daily Mirror* collections *Children as Writers*

not yet been extended to all fields of experience, and there are classrooms where the work in, for example, mathematics or music is strangely out of accord with the pattern of learning established for other fields of knowledge.

We need to consider the nature of 'the discovery approach'. The Plowden Report* describes learning by discovery thus:

> Initial curiosity, often stimulated by the environment the teacher provides, leads to questions and to a consideration of what questions it is sensible to ask and how to find the answers. This involves a great exercise of judgement on the part of the teacher. He will miss the whole point if he tells the children the answers or indicates too readily and completely how the answers may be found, but he must not let them flounder too long or too helplessly, and can often come to the rescue by asking another question. But, though constant dialogue between teacher and children is an essential feature of the approach we are describing, it would be wrong to picture it all as taking place in the class-room . . . Essential elements are enquiry, exploration and first-hand experience which may mean expeditions, perhaps no further than to the playground, but sometimes to a railway station, factory, a wood or a pond.

In mathematics we realize that children need the experience of taking the initiative and thereby developing a sense of personal control in their work. The teacher's explanation, followed by blackboard examples and further verbal instruction related to a particular and isolated technique such as 'carrying' provides a recipe for the child to follow, whereas the discovery approach depends upon a developing dialogue between child and child

* *Children and their Primary Schools:* A Report of the Central Advisory Council for Education (England) (HMSO 1967), paragraph 669

and teacher and child. In the latter pattern children are not merely following the instructions of some external authority but are always partly responsible for their own discoveries.

In mathematics personal discoveries are possible within the field of notational and basic arithmetical ideas. By arranging and operating on items of apparatus a child can discover the nature of the addition process. The discovery is dependent upon the child's own actions with the materials—he gains actual experiences of addition. Similar personal discoveries are possible within the field of pure mathematics. Children respond to a sense of pattern, order and rhythm with such items as odd and even numbers, number series and magic squares. Perhaps the most obvious use of the discovery approach in mathematics is seen in the use, by the teacher, of various problems that have their beginnings in an awareness of the immediate environment.

One or two examples will illustrate the approach of a teacher attempting to develop a range of personal discoveries for the children in his care.

A teacher wishing to introduce the topic of 'area' asks the question 'Which is larger?' and provides a range of irregular-shaped pieces of material in order to generate a concern with the *amount of surfaces*. (The alternative was an instructional situation utilizing regular shapes such as squares and rectangles and the *abstraction* of the experience $l \times b$ *by the teacher*.) The teacher encourages the personal involvement of children in the discovery of a number of possible answers to the question 'Which is larger?' The teacher knows that there will be a groping, experimental period when the children search for examples, solutions and additional problems (largest leaf, largest hand, largest shadow . . .). These activities will be used by the teacher to develop a discussion of various units, tessellations and, in the end, standard units.

The discovery approach is aimed at ensuring that children have a wide and varied experience out of which will come understanding of ideas. The discovery situations devised by teachers generally contain within them built-in incentives to appropriate and accurate computation, and the child's investigations are supported and dictated by the clear and realistic purpose of the problem.

An investigation started by a child's question 'How many leaves are there on the tree?' provides an interesting example of the discovery approach. The children followed up the question and found that 575 leaves weighed 1 lb. This discovery followed three days of counting and weighing and was stimulated by the further questions from the teacher, 'Are there any ways in which we could find the number of leaves on the tree without actually counting every leaf?' The dialogue between teacher and children resulted in a discussion of the question of reasonable accuracy and the arithmetical process of levelling up or down.

This commonplace but fundamental 'how many?' question led to the children posing many similar questions (How many wore coats to school? How many dandelions in the field? How many heart-beats in a hundred minutes? How many steps to London?) which provided self-chosen repetition of the computational processes involved and the mathematical understanding implicit in the original question. This discovery investigation was undertaken, as is so often the case, because of an initial curiosity about a phenomenon in the environment, further stimulated by a well-chosen question from the teacher. This was followed by first-hand experience, and by discussion and refinement of the experimental techniques used. Throughout the investigation the teacher encouraged a wide variety of methods, and it is evident that this kind of use of the environment enables each child to make genuine discoveries.

The teacher's task seems clear:

(a) to develop an appropriate co-operative workshop climate in the classroom;

(b) to scrutinize the experiences resulting from the various starting questions, with the intention of developing a general evaluative framework for this type of investigation;

(c) to stimulate discussion through the teacher's knowledge of the individual's development and the adult's experience of the field of learning. (What is the best way of doing this? Is it reasonable to say . . . Will it always happen? . . . and so on.)

The teacher will need to extend much of this small group and individual experience to the larger unit of the class, and it is important to keep a sensitive check on the nature of the recording process. Again there is a need to carry over into mathematics the qualities associated with other fields of experience; for example, the making of concertina folders, booklets and the other devices associated with environmental and observational work.

It is indeed true to say that the discovery approach is the dominant influence in the learning situation devised by the teacher in the primary school. Much of the work since the publication of the 1931 Report* (the introductory chapters of which are still valuable and worth reading) has been concerned with the working out of this basic belief in practical terms. It has been through this steady development from the early growth signs of the 1930s through to the 1950s with the then Ministry of Education National Courses, and through some of the then training colleges, that a body of practice has been built up. In the last decade it is clear that this influence has extended beyond the schools that might be regarded as the pioneers—the pacemakers and leaders of educational advance. Just how many schools are involved in this pattern of work it is difficult to say, but the Plowden comment 'one-third of the children in primary schools go to schools which are quite clearly good'† might be taken as a rough and ready proportion with a further number of isolated classes within rather fixed and formal schools.

---

* *Report of the Consultative Committee on the Primary School* (HMSO 1931)

† *Children and their Primary Schools:* A Report of the Central Advisory Council for Education (England) (HMSO 1967), paragraph 270

6

Children using books

Television, radio, record players and newspapers affect the lives of young children more intimately than we are, perhaps, aware. The characteristic of this seemingly all-pervasive material is mass production and the need to make a profit. It is idle to take a negative attitude to this climate of mass-produced popular culture, but it is clear that much of the influence is not helpful to the teacher in the classroom. It is also pointless to attempt to compete in providing the stimulus in the classroom on the same terms as the professional agencies at large in our society.

The essential differences between the classroom climate and that of open society is that in the classroom we seek and provide material that will lead to reflection and contemplation on the part of the individual child, whereas our 'pop culture' at its worst seeks for a lowest common denominator response that is limited to the immediate recognition of a crude stereotype. It is this difference in intention between the professional educator in the classroom and the agencies in the open society of children that provides the key to the special place of books in the pattern of work in the junior school.

I began my teaching career in a small three-teacher school where the task of providing visual stimulation was comparatively simple. The present level of visual material was just not available. Not one child in the school had a television set at home, and the possession of a slide projector and colour camera (now almost commonplace possessions) was unheard of. The teacher with a filmstrip projector had an easy task due to the novelty of the situation, and the stimulus of the filmstrip was a powerful support to written and other forms of recording by the children. Now the general stimulus level is so high that we have to do much more than merely stimulate. We need to engineer the classroom situations so that the initial stimulus will encourage a sustained individual or small-group effort and a reflective response.

Of course, the most powerful factors at work in this context will be the pattern of personal relationships accepted and encouraged by the teacher, and the use of direct environmental and psychological experience, but it is also clear that the teacher's role in relation to the use of books is vital.

The careful use of books guards against the 'snippets of information' approach encouraged by so much television. Books can also be used to support and generate an enthusiasm for observational and exploration studies. The first-hand experience of, say, making a brass rubbing will, if it is to be more than a passing physical experience, lead into books and thus to an intermingling of personal experience and secondary source 'research'. It is in this way that a child makes knowledge his own.

The successful use of books by young children depends upon the recognition by the teacher that children (and adults) use books at various levels. We tend to talk of 'reading books' and to expect a certain rather narrow pattern of behaviour in relation to the books.

First we need a sound basic provision of books in the classroom. Books are too important to be kept in a special room at the end of the corridor. The classroom collection will reflect the special curriculum interests of the class and the age group, though some titles included in the basic collection will come under the heading 'too young' for this class as well as 'too difficult'. *The Tailor of Gloucester* will be present in a ten-plus classroom, and so will picture books such as *Mike Mulligan and his Steam Shovel*. Children, like adults, need to range back and forth over their reading experience and the classroom collection should encourage this. Other books such as *The Wooden Horse* exist at different

XI

XII

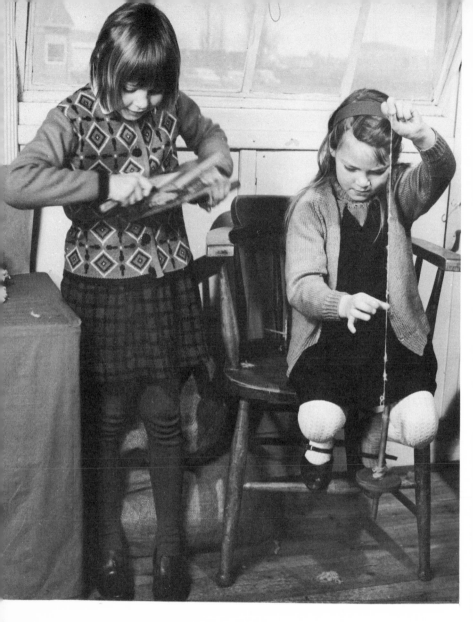

XV *A classroom needs to provide opportunities for working with what can be termed the basic materials of man. Here two children are involved in the carding and spinning of wool that they have collected from the hedgerows.*

levels and the adventure story content for the six-year-old is replaced by the poetic elements for the ten-year-old.

Such a collection of books in the classroom (though not 'classroom books' in the traditional sense) permits a child merely to look at the pictures, to browse, to use a selected page to help identify a flower, to find out more about a topic and, of course, it provides the opportunity to enrich the imaginative experience. It should also be possible for the teacher to turn to this classroom collection to draw source material for class occasions.

If the classroom collection needs to reflect age stages and levels of use, it is clear that each child in the class cannot be restricted to one reading book at a time. He will certainly need a book to hand that can be read easily and rapidly, a book or books to be studied in some detail in relation to a personal or group investigation, and, at times, a book that is a little too difficult for him and has been introduced through the teacher reading extracts to the class.

Books have, of course, a major influence on the quality of written work in the classroom. They provide examples of approaches to problems of collecting and collating material. A child's own book production, through examples of illuminated scripts, decorative margins, cover designs, page layout, supporting illustrations, indexing and so on will be influenced by the book collection in the classroom. It is a strange fact that so many teachers neglect the obvious gain in readability, apart from other aesthetic considerations, when a page of writing has proper margins. One has an uncomfortable precipice sensation when reading 'school writing' that runs to the edge of the page.

Books must come into a positive relationship with the written work of children, and frequent discussion of examples taken from the classroom collection is an obvious responsibility of the teacher. We shall discuss this point further when considering written work.

Books also affect the teacher's view of the curriculum. Immediate small-scale topics to do with materials, buildings, people and events in the environment have a special contribution to make to the curriculum of the junior school. The more traditional local study, though less significant, has a place in the pattern of work. The starting-point often seems far removed from any local study in the accepted sense. It is often a question of a collection of stones or barks from trees from the immediate vicinity, used as stimulus points for design experiences and for descriptive, factual, or imaginative writing, rather than a historical or geographical study.

However some starting-point (say a local mill or bridge) may stir interest about examples beyond the immediate locality, and then the teacher can help the children to develop a historical or geographical study. But we should regard the use of the terms 'geographical' and 'historical' with much caution. The purpose of the work is related to the nature of the experience gained by the children and the historical or geographical material is almost completely incidental to the situation.

Historical material provides an imaginative experience akin to that derived from reading a story and this situation may include some experience of time. The historical theme that runs through a cluster of activities around such a topic as 'Victorian Times' is selected by the teacher because it is a context for an imaginative experience that will range from the minute detail of one family almost within the personal call of children in the class to the reading of a book such as *Lark Rise to Candleford* by one or two of the older girls in the class. Such a patch treatment may spread through much of the term, but it will be rare for such an interest to displace the range of more immediate and small-scale experience derived from the child's intimate relationship with his everyday environment of people, places and things.

From time to time in the life of a primary-school child a more geographically orientated theme will have a place. Again, such a book as Meindert De Jong's *The Wheel on the School* may provide the core for the range of activities that will be taken up by some of the children. The concern of the teacher with the nature of the experience rather than the conveyance of historical or geographical facts should be preserved; it is quite inappropriate to start with a basic subject syllabus with its series of prescriptive comments.

Books, in such circumstances, should provide extensions of imaginative experience (for example, Cynthia Harnett's *The Woolpack*) or technical material (for example, Nancy Bradshaw's *World Costume** or Macklin's *The Brasses of England*†) and observational 'know-how' (for example, some of the Patrick Thornhill booklets such as *Get to Know the Parish Church*‡). The O.U.P. booklet *Fifteenth Century Wool Merchant* is an example of a booklet specially devised for young children and of sufficient quality to make its inclusion in the classroom collection worth while.

Many schools will have inherited sets of geographical and historical textbooks, and though the majority provide an inadequate amount of original source material and inadequate indexing, and are obviously not intended to generate personal response, or work, the material can be made available for reference work. However, group or individual investigations need a range of books specially collected by the teacher and the children and, obviously, the local children's librarian is a potent source of help.

With work of this kind difficulty of vocabulary (a much overstressed factor) falls into the background. Children will read and solve vocabulary problems if the material says something worth while that the children are interested in finding out about. Time and time again such a use of books in a classroom reminds us that young children will use books beyond the vocabulary level supposed to be appropriate for their ages. We so often provide graded vocabulary books with which the young reader cannot

---

* Bradshaw, N., *World Costume* (A & C Black 1952)
† Macklin, H. W., *The Brasses of England* (Methuen 1907)
‡ (Methuen)

reach any significant relationship. There seems little point in insulting the child by contemplating the removal of the word 'soporific' from Benjamin Bunny.

A glance at any publisher's catalogue reveals that the use of information books has changed considerably in the last two decades. The number of information books specially devised for primary schools is vast and some are quite clearly of good quality. Many titles should be available in the classroom collection, but the trend towards the purchase of good reference books (that is, those used by the enthusiasts in the field) that has become more pronounced in the last decade is welcome and provides for a richer and more worthwhile working situation for young children. Flower, fossil and costume identification work requires the best of reference material and there is little point in purchasing the many sketchy and inadequate school books. A child may well use the excellent little school book *Life Before Man*, by Duncan Forbes, but any sustained work on geology will soon take him to a more detailed reference book.

Another welcome change is in the type of information book now being produced for schools. We are moving away from the rather pointless sketchy treatment of 'The Story of Coal' or even 'Ships through the Ages' to detailed themes such as 'Weapons and Armour' or 'Heraldry', with adequate original source material and a stress on observational technique and the encouragement of a working process rather than the mere acquisition of isolated facts. In a modest way some of the original *News Chronicle 'I-Spy'* books provided an early indication of a trend that is now becoming well established.

The present range and quality of books to be found in the best primary classrooms is a far cry from the early days of elementary education in the nineteenth century. At that time the book material provided was frequently in the form of factual items intended for memorization or routine reading practice round the class. The material was not intended for enjoyment or as an extension of the imaginative experience. The knowledge of human development did not extend to a recognition of child development in the way that society accepts today, and little thought was given to the content of children's books. The moral improving tone and the Calvinistic hymn-book were significant influences in the production of books for the young; one Victorian reading primer contained the line 'And his body will soon decay'!

Today the basic stock of information reference books in a classroom probably includes some thirty titles displayed with covers facing the room and a further hundred titles in normal shelving, with their spines forward, as well as an additional collection of rather more frequently changing fiction and poetry. The classification will be informal and in tune with the interests and pattern of usage of the children, resulting in some simple broad grouping on shelves or in corners. The books will be so much an integral part of the life of the class that the children will know the collection (and which child or teacher has borrowed which title!) and will not require elaborate card indexes or filing cabinets which in a classroom becomes so much lumber between the children and the books. Each child will probably keep a list of titles read and thus the need to disfigure books with tabs, date sheets and classification numbers is avoided.

Wherever possible many of the books will be in a library corner (see photograph XII) with carefully chosen furniture and a sensitively arranged environment. A carpeted floor or a rug, curtaining and local lighting, can do much to provide a differently textured environment and many minor conversions of corners of traditional classrooms have been undertaken by teachers and parents working together. With enough space and appropriate school furniture it is often possible to gather the class around such a corner on the occasions where the teacher reads to the class. This simple change in seating arrangement (see photograph I) makes all the difference to the atmosphere at storytime, and it seems almost incredible that many junior teachers still give themselves the almost impossible task of creating an atmosphere for a shared imaginative experience by reading a story to a class of children seated at desks in formal rows. No infant teacher would attempt such a thing, nor for that matter would a professional actor regard this as a reasonable context for such an experience.

The contrast between the use of books in the prewar elementary school and the continued improvement in the pattern of usage in the postwar primary school provides an obvious but significant measure of the changes in intention in the nature of working opportunities offered to children. The classroom collection of books covers different fields of experience from those of the earlier traditional sets of textbooks: there is far more emphasis on observational and what are perhaps rather grandly referred to as 'research' techniques than on items of rote facts as such.

The books are part of the personal experience pattern we seek to provide in our classrooms and the choice of titles reflects our particular concern with heightening the senses and with the gathering of impressions. The titles reflect our special concern with the small scale, the detail of the child's immediate and personal environment and the close relationship between these and the pattern of recording activities—writing, sketching, painting, printing and so on. The books form a vital link in all this, and the published book merges quite naturally into the range of books and other written material produced by the children themselves. Unless this interaction and intermingling of book collection and the activities of the workshop/studio/seminar room/junior 'classroom' takes place, there seems little point in bringing books into school on the scale that we now tend to accept as commonplace.

The discussion of fiction and the realm of imaginative experience involved has been excluded from this chapter, together with rather more detailed discussion of the influence of books on children's writing. These aspects are examined in chapter 10. However, it is clear that the study of local environmental examples, such as bridges and grasses, will lead to purposeful reading and writing. Whilst at other times a story such as *Kon-Tiki* or *The Woolpack* will lead to a term's work spreading far beyond the original content of the story book. *Kon-Tiki* leads to tides, great voyages, great sailors, sea birds, shells, etc., while *The Woolpack* leads to a study of wool, dyeing (experimenting with vegetable dyes), spinning, weaving, farming and geological material (building materials, grazing lands, and so on.

Information or reference books of a wide range and order of difficulty are used by the teacher to create a suitable learning environment. Sometimes the actual starting-point is a personal observation for example of how a particular animal moves; another time it will be a story told by the teacher, and on yet another occasion it will be a television or radio broadcast. In all cases the teacher is concerned not so much with the contents explored as with the opportunities provided for the use of books. Books are used to encourage children to find out for themselves, to extend their knowledge through personal investigation and to extend their ability to learn in a guided situation.

In using books children learn to work with others, and they discover that books will time and time again bring more power to their command. The confident use of books is one of the valuable study achievements of children who have the good fortune to work in the way outlined in this chapter, and it is clear that the nature of the work pattern is such that an essential requirement in every classroom or learning area is a significant book collection.

7

Books from fact to fiction

Our society is inclined towards the information book and the scientific research situation. We have already discussed the legitimate role of information books in the junior school and the interrelation between this type of book and the hobbies, interests and fields of study that merge to form the school curriculum. Enough has been said to indicate the importance of books, and yet we have still to touch upon their most significant contribution to the development of young children. This is the power of books to contribute to a child's ability to shape and partly understand his experiences—of feeling, of imagination, and of situations that reveal fundamental aspects of people's characters and affairs.

There is in the folk tale, the fairy story and the legend a comforting pattern that touches on latent psychological needs, and it is this deeper level that partly accounts for the young child's fascination and delight in such stories. This psychological aspect will be further discussed later in this chapter. Books enrich the child's imaginative life and provide him with events that he may—in imagination—shape and control.

For the fortunate child story-telling begins at home and is bound up with his emotional ties with his mother (or father, or whoever is the family reader). It is this shared moment that goes far beyond the words read. The pattern of reading stories (fed by the earlier tradition, still happily kept alive by some families, of passing on stories through the generations by word of mouth) is, of course, carried on in the infant school. It is unfortunate that in junior schools reading aloud by the teacher seems to be less widespread. It is to be hoped that all children in a junior school will have the opportunity to listen to the teacher reading at least once in each day, so that a close link may be forged between the mother tongue and the printed word.

Children quite naturally reach plateaus in their reading experiences at various times during their life in the primary school. Sometimes this (as in the case of the enthusiasm of some girls for pony stories) is due to the meeting of psychological needs, but at other times it indicates the need of additional support from the adult if the child is to move on to a range of more difficult books. Much of the teacher's reading to the class acts as a beckoning finger to the child and fulfils a vital role in the nine-plus, ten-plus, age range when children have firmly established their initial reading skills.

Discussions of childhood are bedevilled by the differences between social groupings, and when we talk of the extended period of childhood in Victorian times it quite clearly refers to middle-class families. Compared to the Victorian times, childhood is today a fast-disappearing commodity, and whereas childhood reading for the Victorian middle-class child may well have extended to sixteen years of age, today the upper age limit for many is nearer twelve years. Despite the enthusiasm for *Milly Molly Mandy* by some thirteen-year-old girls, the *Mirabelle* type of publication and commercial pressures are the most vigorous pressures on some children and effectively cut them off from any extended period of reading.

Teachers operate in the primary schools with the knowledge that unless children have a rich reading experience in their junior school there will be little likelihood of a meaningful and sustained reading period being established at a later age. Without this communication of the delight and value of reading, which is the purpose of the teacher's activities in relation to books, children at the adolescent stage will be restricted to pop reading material which presents a range of crude stereotypes and oversimple attitudes to personal relationships.

Books stir the emotions and the imagination and enter into the private world of a child—a curtain draped over the side of a table and beneath the table a young child engrossed in 'his book' —his world. The book corner in the modern classroom with its change of textures (carpeted floor, local lighting, curtains and well-arranged books) contrives to produce this subtle environment for the personal and reflective meeting with books, and in so doing captures something of the good home and its special places for children's activities. Absorption is the quality the observer looks for in children and their reading.

The teacher providing books in the first year of the junior school carries over some of the infant books, and the recent flowering in the production of modern children's books for this age means that the only difficulties are money and making a selection from a wide range of picture books. Titles such as *The Cow that Fell into the Canal, Mike Mulligan and his Steam Shovel* and *My Naughty Little Sister*, in which children personify inanimate objects as well as animals, will be included in the classroom collection, as well as books of real incidents within the range of children's knowledge.

Much will have been read to children at an earlier stage, but many will now enjoy reading the same stories rather than having them read by the teacher: *A Bear called Paddington* is one example, and some will begin such books as *Worzel Gummidge*, following the reading of extracts by the teacher.

Within the classroom collection there will be examples of animal stories and here the teacher will seek to provide examples of a more worthwhile kind than the grotesque parodies included in so many cheap books available in chain stores and multiple branches of bookshops. Many seven-year-olds will be meeting Beatrix Potter (*The Tailor of Gloucester* and *Peter Rabbit*) for the first time, and the failure of the writer to observe the canons of vocabulary control will mean that children will have books that are worth reading.

The repetitive recurring situations of the folk-tale will form a significant element in the book collection. The Russian folk-tale *The Magic Glove* will take its place beside *The Adventures of a Little Wooden Horse* and such collections as *A Golden Land* (edited by James Reeves). And, of course, there is a range of simple reading books that will find a place in the classroom: *Sammy the Seal* (The World's Work), *The Cat in the Hat* (Collins) and some of the booklets from the more reasonable 'reading schemes'.

Any discussion of age groupings must be preceded by the establishment of a broad and necessarily crude set of criteria for the initial selection of a basic classroom stock. Given this starting collection, the teacher matches books to individuals and adopts a flexible purchasing policy to meet the needs of individuals. It is with this reservation in mind that we consider the remaining years of the junior school.

For second-year juniors the fable, myth and legend should still be well represented. Nonsense poems such as Eliot's *Practical Cats* take up the earlier delight in

> Doctor Foster went to Gloucester
> In a shower of rain;
> He stepped in a puddle up to his middle
> And never went there again.

and at this stage some ballads and narrative poems are the special contribution to the class from the teacher's reading.

For third-year juniors the myth and legend represented by some of the O.U.P. series forms a vital element in the reading pattern, as does the interest in historical legends and stories of heroes—Robin Hood (Puffin edition) is an obvious example. The interest in nonsense tales continues and (a possible influence of television?) the wild-animal story that is founded on fact begins to be significant. The earlier interest in the small-scale family stories (*Milly Molly Mandy*) is taken over by the adventure story involving boys and girls, providing it has a happy ending. When, for some girls, the pony story becomes an almost obsessional concern the teacher has the task of offering stories that demand a more imaginative element than many of the 'page-fillers' in book-shops. Mary Treadgold is a helpful lead to the teacher seeking a criterion for the selection of stories that will lead to growth beyond the 'page-filler' type of pony story.

By the final year the holiday adventure stories by Arthur Ransome, domestic life and career stories for girls, fictional travel books and a deepening interest in historical fiction (Rosemary Sutcliff, Henry Treece) are important ingredients in a basic book stock.

It is not very profitable to have a static concept of 'children's classics' as a section of one's basic book stock. One advantage of good children's books is that adults enjoy them, too, and we should not attempt to profess a set of children's classics that we cannot personally enjoy. Of course, the interests of a class of forty children will probably be more catholic than those of an adult, and it is not suggested that the book collection should be restricted to those titles the teacher has enjoyed—though this will probably be the case for those selected for reading aloud to the class. We should avoid the prescriptive 'You ought to enjoy this one, it's a classic', but for the ten-plus groups *Treasure Island, Kidnapped, Little Women, Heidi, The Secret Garden, Black Beauty* and others will be available and some of these titles will be enjoyed by each child.

Throughout the years of the junior school there is a need not yet mentioned, that for a small collection of poetry in each class-room—say some twelve to twenty titles above the basic stock of about one hundred and fifty. *The Cherry Tree* (Phoenix) and Walter de la Mare's collection *Come Hither* (Longmans) are two musts. The Penguin publications *Animal Verse, A Puffin Book of Verse, A Puffin Quartet of Poets, Belloc's Selected Cautionary Verse* and the collections by James Britton (O.U.P.) are good sources and relatively inexpensive. The reading of poems will link up with the children's own making of poems, which will sometimes be

individual and, at other times, the result of a small group combining to 'make a poem'.

Books stir the imagination and help the child to retain an open
receptive attitude to ideas, but above all they enrich his imagination and encourage him to extend his awareness of feelings. Books
are in this sense companions, and the teacher, provided that he is
also a reader in the classroom, can join forces with the book and
accompany children into experiences just as valuable as those
arising at first hand.

8

Writing: sharing experience

Writing depends on opportunities for shared experiences, opportunities for conversation, for listening and for discussion. And all this depends upon the pattern of the day and the week for the class and on the school environment. We must recognize the importance of social relationships. Young children are prepared to write because they share events and concerns with their peers and their teacher, and they are prepared to be personally involved in their writing to the extent that they are confident in their social relationships—confident that their writing will be received in a full sense by the 'audience'.

Language development depends on talking and listening to other children in the class and to the teacher. Writing is one activity in this matrix of language, and writing will involve a child's own interests, his social and public experiences and his private experience. A child must believe that his writing will be accepted, respected and understood and evaluated in a way that is significant for him.

The private world of the young child chasing *his* marble through the moving panorama of obstacles in the supermarket provides legitimate material for the teacher to use as a basis for a class exploration of a living theme. The world of grandmas, mothers, puppies and pets, witches and dreams, also provides good material for the child and often helps him to come to terms with a latent psychological problem.

The teacher's role in deciding whether and how to use this material for class writing in a more public context is discussed in chapter 10, but at this stage we must be aware that the teacher cannot legitimately rely upon this private world of the child as the spring of all the writing undertaken. Nor is it reasonable to set up an area of 'free' or 'intensive' writing that relies upon deeper psychological tension as its motive power, and to make a sharp demarcation between this and the traditional range of writing activities associated with school. If the art of writing is to have any significance for the development of the child it must reflect a fundamental acceptance of the primacy of language development, with writing as a closely related activity that grows out of situations that are significant and meaningful to the child. It seems to me that the process of writing is the prior concern of the teacher, and that less attention needs to be given to the results. It is the process that will be discussed in these three chapters, and through this consideration we shall come nearer to an understanding of the imagination and thought processes of young children.

What happens when children are encouraged to write about what they see? There is enough evidence of exciting and sustained writing based on observational studies to make it clear that this is a major ingredient in any pattern of writing activities offered to children. Yet there can be few teachers who have not sometimes been disappointed by results. The difference between success and disappointment for both children and teacher lies in the recognition that the teacher must be deeply involved not only in the actual writing but also in the earlier sensitizing process.

Consideration of the end product alone will not lead to growth. The teacher uses techniques to heighten the observation process. In the early stages before the children are able to bring a rich experience to work the teacher will heighten the process by, for example, disturbing the scale, perhaps by looking at a rock specimen from below table level so that it takes on the character of a towering cliff with caves. Mary Norton with her precise image of a miniature scale provides in *The Borrowers* an example of the universal nature of this kind of sense experience for the creative work of the adult and a young child. The teacher will heighten detail by the introduction of a hand lens or a selective viewpoint (cut-out card frame), or by a contrast obtained by the juxtaposition of textures (shell or rock on velvet) and in such ways concern himself with *sense* experiences. This may seem a point of detail, but any survey of past practice in English teaching quickly reveals that our past preoccupation, if not obsession, has been with the content of the end product; the acceptance of an approach orientated towards the use of the senses does represent a departure for many teachers.

Sense experience in this small-scale simple way provides the raw material for reflection; and the more we concentrate on the impression rather than the expression, the more we help children to realize their experiences. Let us not forget the scale of a child's world—of most significance is what he feels it possible to encompass in his cupped hand.

This work demands a rather special viewing of the classroom environment. We seek to entice, to fascinate, to encourage children to look into the heart of things. We want them to listen more carefully, look more closely and touch more sensitively.

Bark, stones, shells, rusty tools, grasses, all become resources for the teacher, and though they will often not lead to writing, it is clear that the process of looking closely will frequently lead to attempts at sketching and to written descriptions. In the early stages of this type of work the majority of children will not venture beyond the factual description. However, providing the observational work is related to small-scale items and grows out of a generally stimulating classroom environment with aesthetic standards, the balance between factual and imaginative will be reasonable. At times the observational starting-point will be a springboard for personal writing of an imaginative kind, and at other times the factual description will intermingle with the imaginative sequence.

Such themes as cobwebs, early-morning streets, shadows, smoke, houses, noises at night, the wind, the pond, have a clear

XVI

XVII *The arrangement of working bays developed in the DES design for the Finmere school enables the teacher to develop a much simpler and more subtle teaching pattern. Specific areas can be specially designed for clay, painting and similar activities, whilst other bays can be 'textured' to provide stimulus and support for writing and other modes of recording.*

XIX

sense-experience starting-point and the teacher will be active at this stage, ensuring that all members of the group share many of the same sense experiences. But in these instances the observational starting-point (perhaps because it obviously involves more than seeing) is less likely to lead to work that is purely descriptive. This is not, of course, to suggest that the teacher will be disappointed with writing that is purely descriptive.

Written work that describes bark, shells, rocks, grasses and other objects encourages class or group discussion of words and phrases. The task of description is seen as a worthwhile one because of the immediate context, and it provides the guidance the writer needs. Rules need not be considered apart from the task or context. The searching for words and spellings, and the consideration of page arrangement will slow down the pace of the work and encourage reflection and redrafting. It is a time of legitimate experimental trials and draftsman's discussion. Children will respond to the struggle to find adequate words to catch the fleeting moments of observation, and the purpose of the task makes it an exacting one. Both reader and writer can refer back to the object and the purpose of the writing in order to refashion a word or phrase. The 'correction' process is at the drafting stage and is in relation to perceived differentiations of details, rather than to a teacher's set exercise and 'correct' answer.

This type of writing (like all worthwhile writing) has an audience, a reader, in mind. This context gives the work a sharp focus and clarity and is of a different order from the deliberately contrived series of sense experiences (methylated spirit on the hand, keys, and so on) provided by Dora Pym and Margaret Langdon.* The work described in this chapter is derived from a primary-school environment and approach making a much more basic use of sense experience from the day-to-day pattern of work.

---

* Pym, D., *Free Writing* (University of Bristol Institute of Education—University of London Press 1956); Langdon, M., *Let the Children Write* (Longmans 1961)

It is as well to remember that Coleridge never so much as crossed the English Channel and yet we have the images of *The Ancient Mariner*. As Peter McKellar reminds us,* Coleridge's early notebooks reveal that the journals of Cook fascinated him, and we have in *The Ancient Mariner* a combination and re-arrangement of much of Cook's first-hand experience on his voyages.

It seems clear that the creative process is not a simple one, and it follows that we should not expect children to create something original and imaginative 'out of their heads'. The more one reads of accounts by writers of their working pattern the more one becomes aware of the primacy of sense experience, with which secondary perceptions (such as Coleridge's early contact with Cook's journals) are mingled, and the cumulative effect of experience. The rhythm and time scale of the creative process bears no relation to fixed timetables and short periods of work. The teacher needs to set up a work pattern in a classroom that makes it possible for children to try things out, to reflect, to bring other techniques, media and experience to bear on the original stimulus, and then to return to the original 'try-out' piece of writing. It is a simple fact that many children are not given the opportunity to try out words and phrases in draft form in the classroom—yet no teacher would dream of writing a letter of application without several drafts and time taken to ponder and reflect! The author will long remember the surprise of a nine-year-old girl visiting Bleak House and seeing the original much-corrected manuscript for *Bleak House* by Dickens.

The creative process involves a reciprocation between first-hand experience and the secondary experience provided by books. The process demands an imaginative identification with emotions, people and events. Books often act as a yeast, activating and extending the original first-hand observational experience. The resultant deeper understanding of the original

* McKellar, P., *Imagination and Thinking* (Cohen 1957)

experience will often cause the child to return again to the original observation situation.

'Look, this book says just what we have seen about caterpillars eating', can be the start of a more intensive first-hand study.

There has been a tendency for teachers to demand a fixed and far too abstract response to the task of writing. The work already described in this chapter brings the child's situation nearer to the realistic expectations of a writer attempting to create. The key to writing lies in the acceptance of a different pattern and rhythm from that associated with traditional timetables and textbook situations. All who are concerned with providing opportunities for children to write will find Peter McKellar's accounts of Coleridge, Byron and others fascinating and valuable correctives to any undue concern with the end product rather than the process. The Bodley Head Monographs on children's authors such as Mary Norton also provide valuable insights into the cumulative effect of experience and the fundamental contribution to the style of our writing made by the way we see things.

The more limited use of stimulus, suggested by Dora Pym in *Free Writing*,* has a place in the situations provided for writing—more especially in any period of change from exercise-dominated writing to context-based writing. Dora Pym suggests that such stimuli should not be used more than nine times during a year and without proposing an upper limit I would suggest that the need to use such situations more than rarely after a changeover period, is probably an indication that the writing opportunities offered have been too restricted and teacher-dominated. The use of stimuli such as methylated spirit, burning candles and so on needs very careful evaluation if it is not to become a series of unrelated gimmicks.

Of course, the work of Dora Pym* was related to the particular problems of devising a stimulus that would provide a

* Pym, D., *Free Writing* (University of Bristol Institute of Education—University of London Press 1956)

release for those who had lost their fluency or were involved in the rather formal and traditional organization of the so-called 'essay', which was included in many of the eleven-plus examinations. The work of Margaret Langdon (*Let the Children Write*)* and Sybil Marshall (*Experiment in Education*)† are examples of the development of the idea of 'free writing' within the classroom.

In all this work it is vital that we should allow children to use language for their own purposes. In writing, the child is generally sharing his experience with an imaginary listener. The ebb and flow of personal experience is caught in the process of writing and helps a child to bring order to his world. As teachers we cannot afford to be indifferent to the personal experience of the children in our care, and when we receive their writing it is an invitation to share their experience further. Sally writes of her grandmother and it is the experience that the teacher needs to understand if the writing is to be fully accepted:

My Gran, by Sally

She lives in the old people's flats. She lives by herself
except for a budgerigar. She is very fond of her budgerigar and every morning when she gets up it talks to her.
It says, 'Good morning, Mother.'
She has white hair and wears glasses and if she is puffed
out or cold, great tears roll down her cheeks, as if she
is crying, but she's not.
She is very fond of knitting and listening to the radio.
Every Thursday she has dinner with us. She belongs to
a club which meets on Tuesdays. She goes on a lot of
outings from there.

One does not require methylated spirit or burning candles for such writing, but, cautiously introduced, they do have a part to

* Langdon, M., *Let the Children Write* (Longmans 1961)
† Marshall, S., *An Experiment in Education* (Cambridge 1963)

play. They quite clearly offer a loosely structured situation that is likely to involve children in feelings rather than facts. The discussion will not be about 'What is this?' but 'What does this make you think about?' 'What do you feel?' The smell of spices may trigger off some half-forgotten episode and produce a flow of language that will not be worked on or redrafted in any way.

Some children will use the opportunity provided by a candle, velvet, a rusty lock or a scent to write about the loss of their pet, or about cowboys and Indians. The teacher must be prepared for the child to work through an idea or problem, and must see this personal writing in terms of a development over a year or more. Some resources will, with the child's permission, form the core of a shared experience of fears or other special feelings with the whole class.

The thoughtful teacher will take these opportunities—over a period of weeks—to extend the experience through readings from other authors as well as class members. There will be a growing understanding that comes from the knowledge that fears and experiences are shared by others, and there will be an unconscious combining and rearrangement not unlike the process noticed in Coleridge's *The Ancient Mariner*. Into this field of experience the teacher will introduce class themes such as islands, old people, grandparents, giants, fire, wind and secret places through which children will share many ideas and feelings.

The concertina folder or book will provide visible evidence of much corporate concern, group sharing of stories told and individual endeavours to communicate what is of concern to them as individuals. The acceptance by the teacher of the group booklet or folder, and the use the teacher and class make of the work will determine the depth of involvement at any future date in writing about shared ideas and feelings.

Free writing often touches half-conscious and deeply perplexing themes. There is a wealth of psychological tension that will provide the motive power for sustained and powerful writing. Sally's writing reminds us that fathers, mothers, grand-parents, friends and pets are a rich vein of experience and the act of writing will often help the child to mediate the experience. This will happen in any event and teachers need to be sensitive and understanding in their acceptance of the work. What the teacher should not do is deliberately to exploit the emotional experience as a quick way to 'powerful writing', thus betraying a shallow concern for the end product rather than the growth of the child.

Writing as the kind of activity outlined in this chapter arises from a larger context involving activity, talk and a perceived audience. It is one possible response to a task.

The child will frequently turn to writing because the climate of the classroom encourages an interest in and an enthusiasm for writing. The class will have the oral tradition of the teacher reading stories and excerpts most days of the week. There will be the shared experiences and discussions. There will be examples of first drafts, attempts to find the right word and pieces of work still in a molten state well displayed in the classroom. And there will be finished pieces of work with satisfying calligraphy, well-arranged pages and sensitive decoration and illustration. In such circumstances the child will often write because he wants to and most times the writing will gain from the knowledge that it is genuine communication, that there is a context, a purpose and a receptive audience that goes well beyond the vague realization that 'the teacher reads the exercise book'. The value will be recognized by the teacher and shared with the child.

Perhaps one should expect no more from writing, but in fact the act of writing will often enable a child to become conscious of what was previously a vague realization (the adult and the making of a shopping list is worth considering here) and will act as a mediator between private experiences and the understanding that comes from sharing such experiences.

9

Writing: the need for communication

Writing for children must come from an environment and an experience that provide the child with something to talk about. The writing will always begin with experience, and frequently, talk. The language forms are learnt through speech and the extension of communication by writing carries the experience forward. The act of writing will often sharpen a child's awareness of an original experience, but cannot be a substitute for it. If we are not aware of the blighting effect of years of the traditional secondary teaching which takes Latin as its model for category analysis, we may be inclined to give house room in our primary classrooms to the countless series of textbooks of exercises and comprehension extracts.

Other than the possible but doubtful justification of providing occupational material while the teacher rests, there can be no place for this type of material in the workshop/studio situation of the primary classroom. *First Aid in English** is perhaps one of the most widely known examples of the approach to 'English' that is characteristic of the majority of published textbook schemes prepared for junior schools.

The term 'exercises' implies a view of language completely foreign to any meaningful activity for young children. Imagine

* Maciver, A., *First Aid in English* (Gibson 1939)

wanting (or ever needing) to

> Compose sentences each containing one of the follow-
> ing phrases. None of the sentences should be in the
> form of a question:
>
> 1 several of whom   3 by means of which
> 2 in whose reign   4 the youngest of whom

Such exercises deprive the child of the opportunity to seek out
words in relation to his own experience and, within this setting,
to use words as a means of sharing experience. They distort the
nature of language and neglect our knowledge of the developmental stages of young children. Even for young children language is quickly co-ordinated into meaningful and complex
units, and the attention to sounds of the two-year-old merges into
the concern of the three-year-old and four-year-old with words
and phrases, together with simple and complex sentences.
Language as a skill requires attention over all its parts and any
formal analysis is quite out of keeping in the primary school.

The work of Luria,* of Bernstein† with his discussion of the
'restricted code' associated with social class classifications, as
well as the earlier work of Nisbet on family structure, are evidence
of the primacy in language development of social relationships
rather than textbook exercises. The list of words given in so many
exercises provides a stimulus-response learning situation of the
crudest kind, and is bereft of any context clues to an extent that
makes the task almost meaningless and certainly unhelpful. Words
gain everything from context (assuming experience). For example,
what does one make of the word *exercise*? In a formal textbook

---

* Luria, A. R., and Yudovich, F. I., *Speech and the Development of
Mental Processes in the Child* (Staples Press 1959); Luria, A. R., *The
Role of Speech in the Regulation of Normal and Abnormal Behaviour*
(Pergamon 1961)

† Bernstein, B., see footnote on page 14

XX

XXI

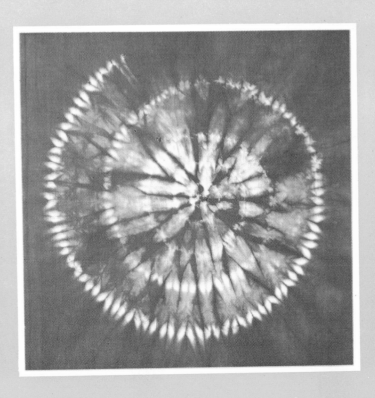

XXII

situation it may well be exercise the dog, or authority or count-less other uses; the context is all important.

It will be a tragedy if the presence of numerous books of English exercises in schools should encourage teachers to con-tinue to teach a series of prescriptive grammatical rules, when it is quite clear that the modern study of linguistics draws its power from logical analysis rather than from any set of prescrip-tive rules. Much traditional grammar is within its own terms misleading and unhelpful and certainly the level of maturity required to handle the categories is beyond the stage of primary education. Teachers in any doubt about the significance of tra-ditional grammar in language work would find encouraging support for the more open-ended primary approach in Frank Whitehead's *The Disappearing Dais** and in F. Flower's *Lan-guage and Education*.† Even in the more traditional and restric-tive view of the educational process there is no evidence available to support the view that primary school children profit from an introduction to such terms as noun and adverb and to the process of categorization.

Writing about 'The difficulty of grammar', Macauley‡ re-viewed the grammar syllabus for Scottish schools. At seven and a half children started a grammar syllabus which involved a period of thirty minutes per day. He tested five classes after five years of grammar, on the recognition of nouns, verbs, pronouns, adverbs and adjectives, and no group reached fifty per cent on the test or in any part of it. The adjective, adverb and pronoun bore no fruit! After six years the picture was even more depressing. Of course, I am not suggesting that the Scottish teachers concerned were inefficient, but that the attempt to teach grammar took no account of the limitations of the children. In England many teachers confess, in moments of doubt, that their attempts to

---

* Whitehead, F., *The Disappearing Dais* (Chatto 1966)
† Flower, F. D., *Language and Education* (Longmans 1966)
‡ *British Journal of Educational Psychology XVII 3* (Methuen 1947)

teach the difference between *too, to* and *two*, or *their* and *there*
merely confuse children, including those who had not until that
moment confused the words. Such are the perils of neglecting
the context!

We have already suggested that an 'exercise' view distorts
the whole nature of writing situations in the school, and that
there is no place for the traditional set of published English
exercises. We cannot have written communication in such an
approach, for writing needs the backing of common experience
and a clearly perceived context and audience. Talking helps to
organize activity and experience and for the very young talk is an
accompaniment to action. A child of just under four will assemble
a series of electrical plugs into a Dalek with the aid of a screw-
driver, and a continuous monologue lasting some ten or more
minutes will accompany the action. The talk comes from the
experience but it has more than an accompanying role. The
young child's statement, 'I must talk to know what I am thinking
about', reminds us of the importance of language. With the
young child many words cannot be used apart from the actual
object or action.

When we use the term 'English' we need a clearer picture in
the mind than that provided by the traditional excess of exercises.
We need to know the kind of activity we have in mind. We must
have an expectation of what will actually happen. The terms
talking, writing, reading and listening are far more accurate
descriptions of events in classrooms.

Spelling and comprehension are two further terms that need
critical consideration. Schonell's work on spelling* takes discrete
items learnt by stimulus-response method as a pattern of learning. We have words grouped on the basis of analysis of sounds:
some silent letter—*knee, knob, knock*; some of a similar visual/
sound pattern—*power, shower, flower*. Again the organic nature

---

* Schonell, F. J., *Essentials in Teaching and Testing Spelling* (Macmillan 1942)

language and the paramount contribution of meaning to our
ech and writing patterns is neglected. The learning of words
olves learning to recognize them in silent reading, learning to
ognize and pronounce them, and, for some words, learning all
s and the spelling.

There is little experimental evidence to go on, but it seems
ar from observations that one wants a classroom climate that
:ourages a positive attitude to spelling and places the work on
individual basis. Each child learns self-chosen words and keeps
ersonal record. The testing can be on a partner basis and need
t involve the whole class. Experimental evidence and observa-
nal experience come together to support the grouping of words
sed on meaning, rather than analytical lists based on sound or
ter abstract categories. Freyberg's comparative study of the
o methods of learning spelling* provides clear evidence on this
int. The Scottish Council for Educational Research† and the
ottish spelling list (booklets published by U.L.P.) has the
vantage of offering groups of words around such themes as the
chen, garden and so on. This is an improvement on the
honell list but for the majority of children greater advantage
uld come if they learned to do the actual grouping themselves.
Comprehension books providing completely artificial situa-
ns serve only to prevent children from bringing significant
mprehension to the wide range of reading and investigational
dies undertaken in any normal classroom. One has only to
: where, other than in a comprehension book, one would be
ected to read an extract first and then the questions. Surely
: ordinary everyday situations of the classroom provide ade-
ate occasion for children to turn to books because they already
ve a question they want to answer. There are one or two books
th rather longer extracts and questions and these provide a
re positive source for teacher and children.

ritish Journal of Educational Psychology XXXIV (Methuen 1964)
A review of research in spelling', in *Studies in Spelling*, by A. C.
atterson (University of London Press 1961)

When we have removed the deadening effect of textbook exercises from the work undertaken by children the nature of the writing tasks can be seen much more clearly by children and teachers. Writing may well at times have a deep psychological significance for an individual in helping him to pattern and recognize the quality of his own private experience, but at all times genuine communication can only come from the establishment of some significant human relationship. The teacher's acceptance of written work, the teacher's contribution through the reading of a wide range of literature (including work by children) and the workshop/studio discussions provide a climate that has a far more positive influence on the quality of writing than that achieved by any number of worked exercises, and preserves the purposeful context. In particular the teacher's spoken example and the use of books in the classroom provides a framework for writing that has qualities of sincerity, directness and an enthusiasm for exploring new ideas.

The craftsman's or artist's concern for disciplined choice, which many textbook writers have misguidedly assumed to be developed by exercises, is, of course, a central concern of the teacher.

The encouragement of choice owes much to our special view of the environment, in which the teacher seeks to bring the children into a heightened visual and tactile relationship with the commonplace natural materials of our world, bark, rocks, metals, grasses, glass and so on. The school is a planned environment offering the stimulus of examples of the best we can provide. Work by the children (sketching, painting, modelling and writing) takes its rightful place alongside examples taken from our cultural heritage, and gains stature in the process by this clear acceptance of its worth by the teacher. The try-out sheets with various attempts at spellings or phrase arrangements replace the all-purpose exercise book, and the buff-coloured composition book, with the county crest, gives way to a range of papers for finished work. Books are made by the children and teachers and sheets of work are displayed. Care is taken with calligraphy and many children are now fortunate enough to have the appropriate tools and examples of a good sixteenth-century hand (the old flexible steel nib and stick penholder, standard to many schools before the war and since, was never a legitimate writing tool.

At this point it is sufficient to indicate that the cursive and Civil Service hands were never in the mainstream of the craft of calligraphy, and the subtle range of varying finger pressures required for good cursive put any degree of style beyond the reach of young children. One of the italic hands provides an appropriate starting-point for the teacher's consideration of this craft skill. The emphasis on experience, coupled with a deliberate intention on the part of the teacher to place much of the written work in the mainstream of the class's shared communication, leads to a greater interest in language, and a sensitivity to the power of language (in this context written work) to encompass experience and to add something to our understanding of observed events, mathematical and scientific investigations, music and painting and the whole range of human feelings.

10

Writing: using literature

It is possible that some teachers do not make a regular practice of reading aloud to their children, but generally we seem to have put behind us the miserable experience of reading around the class or the almost equally dreary pattern of group reading, and willingly accept that the reading of stories to children is essential. The experience of listening to a story is important in its own right for all children, but for the less able reader it is an irreplaceable element and it can provide a fuller imaginative experience than when the child reads for himself. Reading aloud to children can bring them into a relationship with books which would otherwise be too difficult for them, and this helps to ensure that their personal reading does not become fixed at the level of crude character stereotypes associated with Biggles or the work of Blyton.

Such shared reading experiences by teacher and children make a major contribution to the classroom climate in their development of an interest in and enthusiasm for ideas and the imaginative use of language. 'These words go together—they sound smooth.' 'Listen to the sound of this word.' 'That's a wonderful word.' 'That word comes from the French.' Children's conversation often reveals a concern for language based on a rich shared oral experience.

There is no need to make a further case for the teacher's reading books to children; the extension of feeling, deepening of understanding and whetting of the appetite that comes from such an activity is its major justification. But there is another consequence of such a rich pattern of reading aloud, and that is the

mework it provides for some of the writing in the class. The
cher has to be keenly aware of the dangers of working for
ick results and the possibilities of the child producing a rag-
g of borrowed words and situations, but nevertheless it is still
rth while considering the teacher's reading as a context for
ldren's writing.

Out of a pattern of reading—stories, extracts, poems, material
itten by children in the class—comes first a relationship with
people and incidents described, and secondly a feeling for the
ll and achievements of others. By such reading we encourage
eceptivity to the feelings and thoughts of other people, while
arpening our understanding of our own experience. From this
hness of reading to children we take sequences and themes and
ell upon the experiences offered. From time to time the theme
sequences will be taken from the book the teacher is reading
the class (for example *A Bear Called Paddington*, *The Borrowers*,
e *Wheel on the School*, *The Lion*, *The Witch and the Wardrobe*,
e *Railway Children*, *The Stranger at Green Knowe* and *The
oolpack*). On other occasions the teacher will compile a small
llection of brief extracts to produce a cumulative heightening
personal experience of, say, grandparents or parents; brothers
d sisters; night; streets and so on.

From this dwelling on some detailed aspect children gain an
areness of the creative imagination of others and a sensitivity
the imaginative use of language. It is important to see this use
books in relation to long-term planning, spanning several
ms, for it is the cumulative effect that leads to heightening of
nsitivity.

Words will be used by children because they provoke feeling
d thought, help in the patterning of experience and encourage
de-ranging associations. The enjoyment of a sequence taken
om the book being read to the class and the resultant discussion
the vividness of the images and the description, the sound of
rtain words and the general sharing of ideas about the writer
akes a seed-bed for the subsequent activity of the children.

Such talking sessions are comparable to the notebooks kept by Coleridge. (For an introduction to the study of Coleridge's note-books in relation to the writing of *The Ancient Mariner* see the references to Livingstone Lowe's work in *Imagination and Thinking* by Peter McKellar).*

The Bodley Head Monographs on children's authors, for example Rosemary Sutcliff (see page 85) provide fascinating insights into the writing process; and the interest in the sharing of ideas—though the discussions of selected sequences or themes —may be extended to sharing information about writers such as Rosemary Sutcliff and Mary Norton. Such work develops a writer's workshop in the classroom and leads, as already sug-gested, to an appreciation of the skill of others and a heightened awareness of one's own work.

We use the opportunity to read extracts to the class not with the intention of encouraging children to write 'a book of the book', but to concentrate on a particular description of mood, atmosphere or situation. It is not a question of attempting another *Borrowers*, but of sensitizing ourselves to, say, the description of a room as a way of arousing an interest in our own room, and illuminating and extending a child's personal experience.

With young children the folk-story and fairy-tale provide a framework for writing. The repetition that naturally arises from the frequently used pattern of three or seven characters or adventurers allows one to dwell easily upon the minutiae of one of the sequences and avoids any suggestion that the task is to make up a full-length story. A series such as *Living Language* (B.B.C. radio) allows a teacher to choose a set of programmes of particular help with his own plans. The dramatization of *Beowulf* is an obvious example of the power of such radio programmes to provide a rich stimulus, while other programmes present a wide-ranging selection of excerpts.

Teachers, too, are happy to range widely in their readings, and

---

* McKellar, P., *Imagination and Thinking* (Cohen 1957)

such authors as Laurie Lee (*Cider with Rosie*), Dylan Thomas (*Under Milk Wood*), and Flora Thompson (*Lark Rise to Candleford*) will be used along with, for example, the collections of James Reeves (*Golden Land*), Edward Blishen (*Miscellany One*) and a variety of Puffins.

It is obviously pointless to advance our discussion by attempting to make some hierarchical list of suitable books. It is the teacher's understanding of his classroom situation and the children's needs that ensures the richness of literary experience.

Swallows and Amazons will be the starter for one situation, *Beowulf* for another and *The Tailor of Gloucester* for yet another. Teachers gradually begin to rely upon certain sources of information for help in tracking down titles for their classroom collections. Frequently the local children's librarian will be a helpful source of information, as well as publications such as *Growing Point*, *Children's Book News* and *School Librarian*. The teacher's readings will aim at concentrating and distilling an experience, and so an incubation period of a day or more of differing activities will intervene before a child begins to write. At times the writing will be in the nature of a jotter entry or author's notebook, but more often this kind of writing will gain from a clear appreciation of the audience. The writing will have an autonomous quality and exist in its own right, but the desire to share the experience will be revealed in the final shape of the writing—a sensitive concern for page layout, thumb-nail sketches as well as the reading and lively discussion of the work by groups within the class and, frequently, the whole class.

In such situations there is both an empathy with the writer and an expectation about the writing. Children pause in their own work to look in on a group writing—listening to sequences and commenting. There is a clear appreciation of the ideas of others and genuine attempts to understand what others have completed. Children in such an environment point out the work of others and expect that their own work will be read. It is the way his own work is accepted that is most important to the young child and the teacher makes a positive contribution by accepting and confirming the experiences of the children. The teacher extends his concern for his children's work by deliberately involving the class in the process of accepting work so that in the end a child's peers play as vital a part in the pattern as does the teacher.

This is in stark contrast to the beginning of writing for so many children. The young child writes a story and is anxious to share it with his teacher. The whole process of feeling and understanding bound up with the most simple act of communication provides an adequate internal stimulus to further work, but so often the teacher externalizes the process by giving a star for good work. In this way a wrong turning is taken in the early stages and many classrooms provide examples of children who have been forced up this school cul-de-sac by teachers. The satisfaction of seeing one's writing as a mediation of one's own experience is destroyed by such systems as stars and other completely externalized and crude so-called motivational devices.

But to return to our discussion of literature and writing. A teacher's use of literature to stimulate talking and writing, and to clarify experience, is most effective in the seminar-tutorial situation already outlined. Identification with experiences and a widening of understanding and sympathy are the characteristics of the imaginative jump made by children who keep close company with books.

1

;ing teaching areas*

s in the study of the practices of those pioneer teachers who
/e been concerned with developing a basic creative ethos for the
mary school that we see the most significant influence on
,ool design. The period 1945–9 saw the beginnings of school
,igns that did not depend purely on precedent but rather on
understanding of the practice of the most challenging
,ctitioners within our schools. And it is this factor that remains
most vital element in any consideration of school design.
The primary school relies so much more than the old element-
- school on the incidental informal learning that comes from a
ld's meeting with materials, social situations and other stimuli
the contrived enivironment of the school. What the visitor to a
,ool has to recognize is that this pattern of incidental and
ormal learning is one element in a complex range of activity
1 that this pattern is under the control of the teacher. Unlike
: teacher in the elementary school, which was dominated by
,truction and learning by rote, the teacher in the primary school
ognizes that there are many different ways of learning and
ching and that his planning will for the most part involve a

hough the responsibility for any errors must be the author's, the
ebt to David Medd (Principal Architect, Development Group of the
rchitects and Building Branch, Department of Education and Science)
)r his inspiration and advice is gratefully acknowledged. In doing so
would not wish him or the Department to be held responsible for
le personal views expressed.

pattern of varying activities and varying groups. It is a flexible and fluid learning pattern requiring a wide range of materials and equipment. The teacher is anxious to get enormous variety into the small teaching space permitted by current building cost limits so as to involve children in the process of choice within the space framework established by the teacher.

A sensitive control over the surroundings is an essential thread in the work pattern; by appreciating the importance of this control the teacher brings order to what would otherwise be confusion in such intensively used space. Within the framework of the school, space has to be arranged so as to encourage quiet, reflective responses to books and material, the ebb and flow of pairs of children and small groups busy at writing, sketching and other forms of recording, and at experiment and construction activities. The disciplined choice and display of materials by the teacher (apart from all the related and similar work undertaken by children) must be so arranged that the inherent qualities of it are revealed and the sharpness of the revelation is such as to act as a point of fascination, excitement and stimulus.

The complexity and yet essential order of the situation is well described by George Sturt, who, in *The Wheelwright's Shop*,* writes:

I only know that in these and a hundred details every well-built farm-waggon (of whatever variety) was like an organism, reflecting in every curve and dimension some special need of its own countryside. . . .
They were so exact. Just as a biologist may see, in any limpet, signs of the rocky shore, the smashing breakers, so the provincial wheelwright could hardly help reading, from the waggon-lines, tales of haymaking and upland fields, of hilly roads. . . .

* Sturt, G., *The Wheelwright's Shop* (Cambridge University Press 1923)

It is this realization of the organic quality of the environment that leads to a sensitive awareness of the fundamental importance of what we do to organize the teaching areas within the school. The teacher's 'seeing eye' will ensure that the building provides countless examples of everyday objects of good design, well-arranged books and other materials and colours to support a range of work within the building and outside. Above all, wall surfaces and shelves will allow the arrangement of a stimulating mixture of work done by children, intermingled with that done by adult craftsmen and artists. The teacher knows that the everyday surroundings are a vital element in the life of the children in his care and the children will sense and respond to this care for design.

The teacher plans a day in which different activities can take place simultaneously and this enables the child to exercise choice in relation to people, raw materials and selected finished products. The aim is to encourage exploration and discovery by sparking off the imagination. The time-span for each child will vary (even though the teacher will break through and gather together a large group or even the whole school) and the planning is not based on timetables but on the arrangement and use of the various spaces within and without the school. A school design must take account of this flexible pattern and variety of activity and the first obvious change is that the total area of the school is seen as teaching space. The areas are subtly differentiated and provide a gradient of choice of spaces from the small enclosed area for, say, quiet reflective reading, to larger areas for general 'research' and recording activities, and yet larger areas for movement and physical activities. There are smaller covered external extensions for some noisy and messy activities and the school site is used as a study area and as part of the larger teaching area that makes up the neighbourhood—whether it be urban or rural.

If our buildings are to aid and enrich the special quality of learning that makes up the ethos of many of our primary schools, then they must have built-in variety. This variety of character strengthens the relationship between teacher and child discussed in this book.

An elegant design solution to the educational demand for a rich yet orderly environment, and the disciplined arrangement of enormous variety of working possibilities within a small space, is seen in the small two-teacher school at Finmere* in Oxfordshire.

The accommodation consists basically of a series of small working areas (one of them in the form of a covered veranda), all with a certain degree of privacy, but still a part of the whole. Each has a certain character of its own. One area is a sitting-room, designed mainly for younger children. This is furnished as any sitting-room might be, with tables and chairs, including a rocking-chair, a window seat, bookshelves, curtains and a rug; there might have been an open fireplace, but instead there is an electric fire to sit around. A small 'bedroom' alcove, which can be curtained off, has a bed, drawers and mirror and shelf. Three more small areas are furnished as studies, with tables, chairs, book shelves, a wide sill and some pin-board and chalk panels. Two other areas are intended primarily as workshops, and are therefore near the veranda so that materials and work can be taken easily from one to another. They have a fixed work top under the window with a washable plastic finish, a long sink with two cold water taps, shelving, pin-up and chalk-board panels. Another area is the kitchen, with sink, working surfaces, wall cupboards and a small electric cooker. And lastly, there is a library or book area, with tables, shelving, wide sills and curtains and a rug.

The basic contribution to this variety and flexibility of work use was the creation of 'working bays'. The bays offer the teacher the possibility of arranging some of the class in a general teaching area (which is also arranged so as to take the full pastoral group of the teacher) and other groups in the various bays. The teacher working in such an environment has sight lines to all the bay

* 'Village Schools' Building Bulletin, no. 3 (HMSO 1961)

.s and can easily keep in touch with the general pattern of
k while allowing the various groups a feeling of privacy in
r bays; the groups have the advantage of a localized learning
ι that has been specially constructed for craft or cooking or
ary work. The teacher is able to take advantage of the differing
racter of the various bays to plan a work programme for
ups and individuals that has variety and a rhythm over a whole
's or week's work. Such an environment extends the range of
ice open to teachers and children and removes the need for a
litional timetable. Children will work in small groups or as
ividuals for long uninterrupted periods and at any one
nent in the workshop-studio-resource area the observer will
ice a range of activities varying from mathematical investiga-
ιs to tie-and-dye work.

Γhe Finmere Primary School was opened in 1959 and it rep-
ents a distinguished and fundamental contribution to the
ler issue of the nature of environmental design for young
ldren as well as to the particular aspect of school-building
ign. More recently the design for a new three- to nine-year-
grouping, the Eveline Lowe Primary School at Bermondsey in
th London, is a further essay in school planning, but it does
, in the writer's view, provide any new fundamental principles
he kind so clearly demonstrated in the Finmere School design.
ιat it does do is develop the same principles for the larger urban
ool and stresses the co-operative sharing nature of the school
nmunity. Those teachers who have had experience of teaching
various arrangements of vertically grouped children will
ɔw of the advantages that stem from younger and older children
ιring experiences with each other, and the Eveline Lowe design
ιstrates that such clusters of children are possible within the
ger urban school. Indeed, the traditionally rather firm lines
ιt mark off nursery, infant and junior schools are very much
ιrred by this design. As teachers we need designs that allow
chers to share with teachers and children to share with
ldren. This was a fundamental design principle in both the

Finmere and Eveline Lowe schools.

The opening up of the school building to make easily possible the sharing of experience between the various changing clusters of children has led some architects and administrators to suggest the completely 'open plan' school. The teacher would then be expected to give 'texture' to this environment through the deployment of portable furniture. In the author's view this would be an unfortunate development and neglects the essential ingredients of a primary school.

These requirements are unlikely to be overtaken by time or by revolutionary methods. What is always in question is the relative proportions of the ingredients for a given set of children and teachers, and the amount of sharing that is acceptable. If we isolate such basic activities as the use of clay or paint, it is obvious that they require a specially designed area. If we agree that the child's relationship with the world is such that he will from time to time need quiet, restful and secure areas for reflection and thought, then obviously we need to provide appropriate areas. It is in this way that one builds variety into the school design. From the teacher's point of view the challenge of a completely undifferentiated area is likely to result in everything being reduced to a uniform level of stimulation and a steady decrease in the number of rearrangements of furniture. If everything can be moved, probably nothing will be moved.

Easily overlooked in any crude response to an apparently fashionable concern with open plan is the prime importance of a sense of appropriate scale and security for young children. The scale of building should be domestic. The periods and areas of calm and serenity that are such an important element in the experience of children can be lost in the overwhelming impact of open plan, which does not provide a range of contrasted areas related to the more generalized open spaces.

There are, of course, problems that are not completely solved by designs such as the Finmere and Eveline Lowe schools in which groupings and clusters of children are possible, nor by

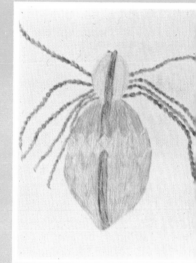
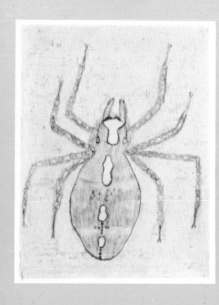
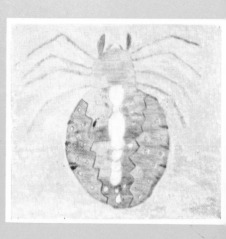

others that have followed, demonstrating different degrees of sharing. It is clear that, though one can build in variety, the space allowed for new schools by cost limits is such that there is inevitably a conflict of needs. There is the need for groups smaller than the whole class (and even worse, the whole school!) to be able to watch television programmes. There is the need for more facilities (particularly with the older primary children) for the use of radio, tape recorders, filmstrip projectors and such activities as the developing and printing of photographs.

Assuming that additional money for a more generous provision of space will not be forthcoming, the space occupied by the 'school hall' in many designs should be reconsidered. The efficient use of this area has been hindered in many areas by the provision of wall and other apparatus for physical education. Much of this fixed equipment could, with design modification, be placed outside the building, possibly with a light plastic roof to provide some shelter. Structural walls could have some kind of climbing challenge built into them, and this, together with some variation in floor level, should be the only design recognition of physical education.

The movement work which is fundamental in the development of children requires a good floor surface. This, in my view, is a priority use for the floor area, but all other physical education involving climbing, ropes and fixed equipment should be outside the main school building.

Just as we have devised sheltered areas for clay, for the study of plants and pets and woodwork, so we should now open up the immediate area of the school to provide a more worthwhile challenge for the physical activity of children. We already contrive window views of the outside world, giving an opportunity for the observation of rain, sunlight, clouds, trees, birds, streets, roofs and smoke. Our doors lead to extensions of experience with ponds, sample study areas and facilities of the adventure playground type. To move out the fixed apparatus is merely an extension of this.

The extra space now available within the school building can be used in various ways. The movement work has a first claim on the floor area, but there is no reason why some areas should not be raised some six to eighteen inches from the basic floor level. Some of these surfaces could be portable, others fixed. Some would be carpeted, others would have wood surfaces. The fixed areas would provide storage for paper in an arrangement similar to the plan-chest storage cabinet. These variations in level would encourage the use of the hall by small groups for drawing large-scale plans of the area, reading, and the use of small portable television sets or radios. At least part of the hall area would become an additional study area that could be used at some stage of most days. Moving the fixed apparatus from the inside of the building would make possible a fresh look at the height require-ments, and this in turn might lead to the provision of extra space. Another possibility would be the provision of a gallery with sound-proof cubicles for music and small group use of radio and television. We need to find ways of making sensible use of a com-paratively large teaching area. Many of the advances in design have come as the result of studying teachers at work in un-favourable circumstances who have overcome the limitations of their building; certainly many teachers are now finding that the hall space needs to be used more intensively.

Architects involved in the development of school designs have used the evidence provided by teachers who have contrived ex-cellent working arrangements with unpromising buildings and furniture. Perhaps the majority of teachers in England can claim at least a brief period in the three-decker castle buildings of the old London School Board. Most survived the 1939–45 war and only in recent years has the crude and insensitive urban renewal with its vast number of tall housing and office blocks over-shadowed their contribution to the London skyline. There is no doubt that there is a rigidity about their floor plan that has daunted many teachers, though there is adequate evidence from teachers who have adapted their rooms to show that much is possible. The Plowden/Architectural Association competition for remodelling a school, and the before and after plans of the Wigton Thomlinson Junior School, Cumberland, are examples of adaptation involving local authority expenditure, though some of the ideas (like those for the new school designs described in the *Building Bulletins*) are suggestive to the individual teacher who is working on a small scale with minor modifications. The beginning of this emphasis on design and the encouragement of changing groups of children, the development of a more co-operative and open community was seen in the design* for the Junior School at Amersham, which was opened in 1958. Here we also see the development of external areas with the planting of shrubs, the creation of quiet paved areas with seating and points of focus, such as a pond together with other outside study areas.

We have now reached the stage when our school building at the primary stage excites interest throughout the world and is witness to the increasing interaction between educational principles and practice and design. The fact that all this has been achieved against the background of a strict imposition of cost limits since 1949 is a tribute to the care and thought that has gone into much of our design work.

The design of schools quite obviously must involve a total appreciation of the situation and this has led to a concentration on the design of furniture placed in the school. The early work undertaken for the Amersham School design (see *Building Bulletin No. 16*) has now resulted in a range of standard units being offered to schools. The designs were undertaken in the belief that developments in educational practice and primary school planning were not being matched by developments in furniture. The new 'Forme' designs marketed by Pel Ltd offer self-supporting movable bench-tops under which can be placed mobile storage units. The range has a variety of working surfaces for sitting and for

* 'Development projects, Junior School Amersham', in *Building Bulletin*, no. 16 (HMSO 1958)

standing height, mobile storage and display trolleys of different kinds and a range of wall treatment items for storage and display.

Thus one has a variety of items which, due to the harmony derived from the recognizable dimensional, colour and material relationship between all the items, avoids the creation of fussy interior character. The range has been designed for use in the traditional closed box arrangement classrooms, or in the more recent school designs that use a series of interconnected spaces.

The teacher has the opportunity to extend the good design of a school building into the detail of the building. The school environment will be an example of good design—good because it works well. Into this context the teacher will introduce a richness of experience involving materials culled from friends of the school, museums and craftsmen and will bring this richness into a disciplined relationship with the wide range of work produced by children. In practical detail this involves the detailed consideration of display, the arrangement and use of the various working areas and the use of storage facilities. Furniture based on these designs is now commercially available through Pel Ltd, Oldbury, Worcestershire.*

Of course teachers will still need to be on the look-out for examples of craftsman-made furniture such as rocking-chairs and upholstered chairs for a reading corner, or for other special needs within the school. This will do much to preserve the growth points in our schools. It is essential that teachers should accept personal responsibility for selecting many items of furniture.

The teacher has to accept responsibility for his working environment if he is to develop to the full a pattern of social relationships and richness of work for the children in his care. Like the good craftsman, the teacher must ensure that his working area has a standard, a rightness and a ship-shape quality.

To evade responsibility for this wide view of one's responsibilities is not, of course, to evade the consequences. A *laissez faire*

* Catalogue available.

attitude means that the teacher will, inevitably, be offering an impoverished standard of visual design example to his children and encouraging a growing insensitivity in them. Perhaps an example taken from a traditional school setting with the traditional view of the school and its 'playground' will make the point clearly.

The traditional flat area of black asphalt in an urban playground is familiar enough. A head and I were standing at the window of a staff room that overlooked a London playground. Looking down at the masses of racing children, he said, 'That's what they need—a place to rush around in and let off steam.'

A few children were standing in the shadowy edges of the playground, but generally the head's comment seemed reasonable in the context of the situation. Boys with their coats buttoned like capes around their necks 'rode' their horses. Others seemed content to merely run up and down the playground, while a few boys attempted to push their way into any more settled game or skipping group.

The following day I was in a school of similar size and it was also true that a number of children were letting off steam on an area of asphalt playground, but in this school it was the range of activity rather than the similarity that particularly struck one. In a partially enclosed courtyard area some children were sitting and reading, groups were sitting and apparently doing nothing, groups were involved in intricate stepping games in an area of differently shaped concrete paving slabs, groups were running up and down a series of varying levels made by a brick-built shape, groups were working in a sandpit (not by any means the youngest) and groups were tending the animals that were kept in the veranda extensions of the enclosed teaching areas. One could go on with the catalogue of activities, but the intention behind this designed provision of opportunity is clear. The view that guides the planning of the internal arrangement of the school has been extended to the outside. Outside as well as inside one should provide a range of rather smaller-scale areas, each with a different character which will probably elicit varying responses. The outside like the inside becomes an area where one is challenged to exercise choice. The fact that it is a school situation means that the choice will be within the appropriate limits devised by the teacher as a result of his professional understanding.

12

A pattern of work

'Please, sir, I've finished my painting. Can I have another sheet of paper?'

Most young teachers can remember with dismay one of their first painting lessons when the young painters were asking for more paper almost before the distribution of paints was completed! The reply 'Use the other side' may well have gained for the teacher a moment or so of respite—but it did nothing to tackle the fundamental problem.

One obvious consideration is the nature of the experience provided and another is the range of materials supplied; but in this chapter it is intended to limit discussion to a consideration of the rhythm and patterns of the work. In the immediate postwar period a casual visitor to many a primary classroom would have been aware of the physical nature of much of the activity taking place. There was a bustle, and indeed often a rush, which showed class enthusiasm, but did not present evidence of a wide range of individual responses. The then popular project was, generally, a rather crude subject-grouping which often did no more than provide a framework for work done by large groups of children. The majority of decisions were taken by the teacher.

Today, we start with a consideration of individuals and of much smaller groups of children and we use our understanding of their needs and interests to develop a much wider and more sensitive pattern of work. We are careful to make a distinction between activity and experience. When we use the term experience we evaluate the impact of the activity on the child. An experience changes the learner in some way, whereas an activity may be merely carried out. Tightening a screw on some machine in an assembly line is an activity, but it is not likely to do much for the worker or to involve him deeply. On the other hand, making a pot or painting a picture involves more of the potter or painter's personality and the activity can be seen as an experience.

The visitor will be impressed by the entirely different quality in the rhythm of the day. With the experienced teacher it will be quite usual for a child to spend the whole of the morning painting, while another child is writing, with all the children following a menu of activities which involve different time spans and different work rhythms. The experienced teacher will have a pattern of planning that, for some aspects of the work, covers the period of a week and, for other aspects, periods of up to a term. Into this basic pattern he sets his own contributions to the class and, of course, his numerous positive interventions which are related to individuals and to groups. Planning, contributing and intervening depend upon the teacher's close observation of growth points.

The problem for the young teacher is to become sensitive to the varying work rhythms of individual children and, in the first instance, to know how to slow down the class pattern in order to obtain control of the work situation. There are many ways of doing this and the following comments are no more than suggestions.

The first task is to heighten the child's appreciation of the craft element in his work; this means that the teacher must consider very carefully the exact nature of, say, the writing situation. A number of details immediately spring to mind. For example, the printed page has margins which give a satisfying proportion to the page and which help it to be read more easily. There is, too, the craft tradition of border decoration using letter forms or pictorial motifs and examples of good book design or thoughtful page layout are readily available.

All this provides a range of example and choice that makes for a richer working situation than the all too frequent exercise book task. Children become fascinated by and very much involved in such a task, and the enrichment of the work both extends the work period (thus for the teacher slowing down the rhythm of the day) and the number of opportunities for teacher-guidance, discussion and so on. Obviously this is not an appropriate approach for all the children's writing, but in the early weeks with a class it is a vital element in changing the pattern of work from a series of teacher-dominated tasks of comparatively brief duration to a pattern of individual and group work allowing the selective intervention of the teacher.

Once the teacher has introduced a basic working pattern for much of the written work (accounts of model-making, sketching, observational work, some stories, the making of anthologies and so on) it is possible to use the time gained to plan some sort of cafeteria system for the day or week. At first the young teacher may well wish to restrict the number of variables in the work programme at any one moment; progress beyond this stage will be a very individual matter and quite clearly partially dependent upon the total school climate.

Just as with certain aspects of writing (we have left out of this discussion the more personal and imaginative elements) where we concentrate on the depth of craft experience available in the simple task of producing a written account, and thus enrich the process, so in the field of sketching we can deepen the experience in order to provide a range of work patterns for the children in our care. Using observational stimuli, sketching and writing merge in the various displays and booklets which are produced in the studio, resource and reference area and workshop, although the twigs, shells, grasses and other items in classroom displays will be used in their own right to generate work that demands sustained periods of activity.

The sense impressions resulting from observation will often be heightened by the use of such things as the hand lens or other devices aimed at isolating and throwing into relief things that are frequently unnoticed. Some of this observational work will involve making close copies, but what we really seek is the encouragement of observation that involves the entire person. Children rarely just look: they look with feeling and this is seen in their writing, their sketching and painting.

Already the young teacher who is planning the pattern of work for his or her class has, with this view of writing and sketching, the possibility of developing an entirely different sequence of minor work periods within the major work period. The extension of possibilities of choice in such basic recording activities as sketching and writing changes the nature of the time unit from the relatively short period to rather less differentiated and longer individual units of work. There is not only an extension of choice but a changing emphasis in the nature of the work. Instead of being concerned with blackboard notes and ready-made second-hand abstractions first-hand sense experience is stressed.

In this lies a great difference from what one found in the earlier postwar primary schools. What may be loosely termed 'the period of projects' was notable for a vast mass of illustrative and painted material in classrooms and a mass of children's writing, generally gathered together in large sugar-paper books and often hung round the walls. In this sense there was no lack of perceptual stimulus and yet the result was that the children remained curiously inert.

Today the teacher aims to achieve greater sensitivity and selectivity in the classroom environment. The meeting of this concern and the children's work is seen in the various situations where the child is working within a very definite, restricted context. The acceptance of, say, making a painting using only one colour or sketching using black paper and white crayon only is an obvious example and, just as with print-making with one colour, the restriction is seen to lead to greater detail of observation and a deeper exploration of the material.

The sensitive introduction of such a technique into the work pattern of the classroom has a significant effect upon the time spans of the work of the children.

For many teachers the factors already outlined will lead to (or, indeed, will be parallel to) a consideration of the untimetabled day. Broadly, this means that individuals and groups have a menu of assignments for the day or week (with developing experience of this way of working, some children will follow assignments that span the term or even longer) and that the teacher decides on an organization that spreads such activities as painting, writing or mathematics over the day and which results in a range of activities taking place at any one time. At nine o'clock one group will be painting, another group writing and sketching, some reading and others busy at a mathematical investigation or exercise. Towards ten o'clock the morning assembly will break into the pattern of individual and group-based work and this may well be followed by a class lesson on some particular skill or technique, or a sharing of some of the work already in progress in the class and used as a growth point by the teacher.

Such a pattern (and this brief description must necessarily be a crude one) reveals an impressive level of professional competence on the part of the teacher which makes sense of any use of 'aide' or other additional help by the teacher controlling this complex pattern. The pattern outlined is, increasingly, the basic element of experience in training courses, and its growth is very clearly nurtured by many talented teachers in schools, who give freely of their time to teacher groups and informed meetings to share this experience.

It is unfortunate that the various B.B.C. television series on aspects of human development have yet to record this pattern of work successfully as case study material, but we have certainly reached the stage when it ought to be attempted. We are also in need of descriptive accounts of the process of change from more authoritarian-structured classrooms to those where co-operative work and the development of children is a vital criterion. Such accounts would do much to share on a wider scale the professional expertise that is already available in probably rather less than a third of our primary schools. Such case studies depend on a firm acceptance of observational technique as the fundamental tool of educational research rather than experimental methods. Miss Gardner's account of the pattern of interventions of the infant teacher in *The Role of the Teacher in the Infant and Nursery School** and its list of some ways of approaching children during the day illustrates the complexity of the teacher's role and suggests the nature of the descriptive work we require.

The pattern discussed supports the social engineering role of the teacher in his attempts to provide a model of the good home, brings into the basic pattern a thread of social and co-operative relationships, and uses the emotional and feeling elements of human experience in the learning context. The school becomes a richer place, offering a greater range of choice for the child, and the teacher's concern with the process of working provides a similarly enriched work pattern. Because there is a greater opportunity for discrimination and personal decision-making, the whole time scale of the work undergoes a fundamental change. The observer is struck by the feeling of calm reflectiveness present in the classroom.

The greater opportunities for choice, and thus variety of response, are reflected not only in the organizational use of the idea of an untimetabled day but in the range of room features and designs. The work by the Department of Education and Science's Architects' Developmental Group is well known and we now have variations in floor level, wall finishes, floor surfaces, lighting levels, work surfaces and furniture as accepted elements in our planning of new schools. But every teacher has a smaller range of possibilities open to him in his classroom and part of his planning of opportunity lies in a fluid use of his working area. Displays, corners where adult members of the community can take part in

---

* Gardner, D. E. M., and Cass, J., *The Role of the Teacher in the Infant and Nursery School* (Pergamon 1965)

the life of the class by talking with small groups, demonstrating a skill and so on, arrangements of books, writing and other work materials together with mathematical and scientific experimental materials, all form part of the patterning undertaken by the teacher. Probably it is the provision of natural materials and books that most readily reveals the influence of the teacher—and it is the influence of the teacher that we really need to consider.

Teachers in primary schools accept the responsibility for the imaginative and sensitive control of the classroom. In practice this means the development of an unobtrusive sensitivity to the countless items that go to make up the classroom day. Much of this work has a wider educational framework, but some of it may be fairly described as organizational routine. More fundamentally one can see that the beginnings of work for young people are to be found in the pattern of social relationships they are involved in. And it is with the quality of social relationships that the teacher is first concerned. In the years that have intervened since the publication of the 1931 Report there has been an increasing emphasis on the power of co-operative patterns of relationships, rather than the competitive situations associated with much of the traditional formal school situation. Miss Gardner's comment on the Plowden Report is valuable:

> The Report, however, does not make the mistake of overstressing the competitiveness of the seven-to-eleven-year-olds and under-estimating their capacity for co-operation which the psychological chapter of the 1931 Report (excellent as it is) is rather inclined to do. In 1931 no doubt witnesses had not had as much experience as we have of observing children of this age working together in creative enterprises.*

'Working together' provides an apt summary of so much of

* 'After Plowden', in *Bulletin* of the University of London Institute of Education (summer 1967)

our attempts to pattern the day and, if we add the nurturing of individual ploys, we describe the nature of our organizational approach.

The purpose of our organization is not to reduce our educational provision to what we can hold in the mind at any given moment or to restrict our interventions to those that can be encompassed by a curriculum statement based on specified and limited 'educational objectives'. Organizational devices that work merely because the choice is limited may have a temporary justification, but ought not to become the basic system within a school or classroom.

13

Organization

Primary education reveals at the nursery-school stage a complexity of human activity that is recognized as the motive power for its organizational pattern. Within the one nursery class unit one sees young children close to their world and fully involved in their talking, painting, building and the play of the home corners and play areas. The young child is in close relationship with the people, things and events that make up his environment. The teacher does not attempt to come between the child and his world but, rather, acts as a mediator.

In such circumstances it is impossible for the teacher not to realize the importance of the task itself for the child and, for example, the idea of some external reward system is seen to be a depressing factor in the situation. One girl on transfer from one infant school to another came home complaining that 'My teacher spoilt my story today.' In fact, the teacher had rewarded the child with a 'a star' for the story, instead of looking with the child into the nature of the internal situation itself. It is in such small but fundamental ways that school organization can develop into a barrier to the full involvement of the child in the activity.

The particular feature of recent educational development within the upper two years of junior school has been the attempt by teachers to use the total involvement revealed by the young child in the nursery school as the starting-point of any consideration of the curriculum, rather than a deceptively simple outline of the curriculum in subject terms. The complexity of human activity observed with young children is now seen and encouraged in organizational terms at the upper end of the junior school. It is this movement away from the boring pattern of the project and its associated 'public relations' type of writing, the lack of variety in classroom activities and the sameness of recording that is, in the writer's view, the most significant growth point in the contemporary junior school.

Every class situation has to be judged for its true significance against a pattern of situations that stretch both back and beyond it in space and time. The skilled teacher *can* recognize the pattern and engineer developments, but he does so with the enthusiastic acceptance of the complex nature of the classroom situation. The aim of organizational devices must be to enrich the pattern of complexity rather than—as so much of our educational research does—simplify through considering ideas out of context.

Whitehead said, 'The problem of education is to make the pupil see the wood by means of the trees.'* It is this view that leads to an understanding of the primacy of the sensually appreciated environment with the teacher's most important role that of heightening the *process* of sense impact. The earlier nursery stage of primary education provides adequate and obvious examples of the part played by imitation in learning and it is this acceptance of the importance of the teacher's being 'of influence' that allows the development of a teaching pattern that largely depends on the teacher 'coming alongside' the child. Education, as Professor Morris reminds us, 'is neither doing things *to* people nor *for* them but *with* them'.†

Any discussion of organization needs to be considered against the background of growth points of education present within our schools. Organization details such as the untimetabled day lead to working patterns where the child is much more involved in exercising choice. The teacher with his attention to craftsman's standards of calligraphy, page and border arrangement slows down

---

* Whitehead, A. N., *The Aims of Education* (Benn 1932)
† Tibble, J. W. (ed.), *The Study of Education* (Routledge 1966)

XXVI *The use of corrugated card helps to break up a square bay into varied working areas. It provides display space and textural variation. The removal of much of the unnecessary furniture gives more floor space for the kind of investigational work illustrated. The boy is using a 100 number ladder for his mathematical task.*

XXVII *'neither doing things* for *people nor* to *people but* with them'

the process of work so that the child becomes aware of the minutiae of choice at the various stages of writing, drawing, painting and so on. Even the question of the appropriate size and type of paper becomes a situation where a child *wants* to exercise choice.

The freer, more flexible programme recognizes the central contribution to our understanding of children from the child development studies over the decades. Early work within the field of child study led, with the youngest children, to an emphasis on the grading of materials for individual children, emphasis on activities and the importance of concrete experience. There is in a general sense a psychological rationale for much of the teaching in, say, reading and mathematics. But even more important for the junior schools is the concept of human development rather than child development. A knowledge of psychology ought, from a teaching viewpoint, to be related to a developing and deeper understanding of what we conceive that we are about when we are teaching. Most important is the insight we gain about the major role of the teacher in making and sustaining personal relationships. It is this readily accepted importance of personal relationships that is seen as a generating force for much of our organization detail.

The psychological background of our work leads teachers to organize, in terms of individual and small group activities, self-chosen tasks using classrooms and school space in a differentiated way so as to develop a diversity of texture experience, resources and usage. There is an organic view of the classroom environment where the teacher engineers environmental pressures, there is a social context to all our work and, above all, there is a generally accepted view of people and human development. One practical example will illustrate the appproach implied in these comments. For years past there has been the custom of a staff meeting called to discuss points of detail, subject content and control of materials in the schools. Today many schools seek to advance their work in the various fields of knowledge through the case study staff meeting. The regular pattern is for a year group (in the case of a large school) or the whole school to gather material together for three to four individual children and through a staff conference on case study lines to advance the broad objectives of the school.

The importance of considering the total context in relation to patterns of organization is seen with the development of family grouping over the past few decades. From about 1945 onwards many infant schools in Bristol were instrumental in the spread of ideas about family grouping as an alternative to the straight age grouping of reception and other classes through the infant school.

Family grouping as an organizational device recognizes the importance of social influence in education and for its success depends upon an adequate pattern of individual and group work within the field of curriculum experience. Family grouping recognizes that the basis of the classroom work is individual and willingly accepts the difference implicit within any group of people. The reception class disappears and the new entry takes his place in an established community. Generally there are no more than four to five new entrants to any one class. Within this complex unit a child will have the opportunity to experience different social roles and to be part of a varying and changing work pattern.

The teacher will have the opportunity to plan her day so as to involve the maximum use of her knowledge and time in relation to the varying needs of children. With such a flexible programme it is easy to see that an older reader will spend a short time with a less mature reader and in so doing gain experience of oral reading in a significant and meaningful situation. In the same way a group painting or a group making a model will make different demands upon the teacher than a group busy counting. The success of the teacher in this situation lies in the recognition that the complexity of the human activity allows different levels of intervention and does not face the teacher with the impossible task of supervising thirty-nine children at reading or doing number. Given a sensitive understanding of the development of children on the part of the teacher, the consequence of this is seen in a rich and differentiated pattern of experiences. Vertical grouping is then seen to be a successful pattern of organization that enables both the teacher and the individual children in the class to be a significant influence in the learning that takes place.

A lesser number of junior schools have attempted a modification of vertical grouping (leaving aside the many excellent small village schools that have no option other than to work as a vertical group) whereby the first two years are grouped together and there are separate nine-plus and ten-plus year groupings. Others have family groupings in the junior school with a lower junior family group and an upper junior family group. There seem to be many advantages in this pattern, but the order of changeover is important. Any change to such an organization must depend on a staff understanding of the situation and come as a response to the desire to increase the number of possibilities open to the teacher and the children.

Certainly it is clear in general terms that the junior schools have yet to solve the problem of encouraging the older and more able child at the top end of the schools to spread out beyond the limit regarded as normal in the present situation. The sustained work and depth of involvement so noticeable in the early stages of the junior school have yet to have a full flowering in the upper school. With the abolition of the eleven-plus examination the depressing effect on the teacher's expectations should gradually be replaced by a more open-ended view of the work undertaken by children in the final year of the junior school.

It is unfortunate that some see the solution to this problem in the modification of our school structure so as to allow the development of the 'middle school'. Given that all age groupings cause some difficulties, the age range nine to thirteen nevertheless seems to produce the greatest number of difficulties in any school organization. It is hard to know why the 'middle school' is seen as a practical solution. It would be far better to consider the creation of sixth form colleges, and opening up the established further education opportunities for older adolescents.

Richness of work in the final year has been largely stunted by preoccupation with content-orientated questions for this age group. Discussion of the curriculum has been dominated by specialists. This has had the effect of lessening the teachers' close awareness of the children's world, and consequently much of the work introduced has not had the powerful incentives for learning available to those who believe in a child-centred approach, and appreciate the value of wholeness experience. It is because of this problem that organizational ideas about family grouping for the older children in the junior school should come as a result of a desire to open up the curriculum experience. In any event such organization changes imply a different role for the teacher.

Much of the discussion of actual organization is advanced in terms of 'free day' or 'integrated day'. It is important to see these terms in relation to the general trend towards opportunities for greater choice on the part of the child. Indeed, it is important to bear in mind that the increased opportunity for choice and an individual rhythm of work is the spur towards what is, essentially, an untimetabled classroom situation. Given this the use of such terms as 'free day' or 'integrated day' may well be misleading or unhelpful. Within such an organization the child largely determines his own pattern of work for the day (gradually the time scale is extended) and chooses the nature of the activity he wants to follow. With this approach to teaching the teacher injects class experience such as the reading of a story or the discussion of a class idea. But in the main the teacher is acting as a guide and consultant to groups and individuals.

In the writer's view the use of the term 'free day' is too emotive for profitable discussion and there seems much to be said for the use of the term 'untimetabled day'. This starts with organizational pattern that provides long stretches of untimetabled work. In the early stages children see this in terms of half a day, then a day's programme. Later this becomes a week and later still the term is seen as the basic unit for much of the work. Into these working periods the teacher introduces his or her own particular class contributions, but otherwise acts as a consultant, master craftsman, instructor and so on to groups and individuals. The teacher also has a major responsibility as a social and environmental engineer. The organizational changes gain their significance from the total context of the classroom that now provides the differentiation formerly provided at a very crude level by the subject divisions of the timetable.

The classroom has varying textures or resources and stimulus areas that can only be adequately described through the use of a chain of terms such as studio, workshop, reference area, experimental area and so on. The introduction of areas (frequently bays) and the control of raw materials becomes a highly significant and selective influence at the command of the teacher. The choices exercised by the teacher in relation to materials and starting-points are a positive influence and lead to a weighting of situations that cause children to experience a sensually appreciated small-scale environment ('seeing the wood by means of the trees') and the reflective, feeling response to the world. It is of a different kind to the series of rote items in the instruction-based curriculum of the old elementary school. It reveals a view of people as people and not as instruments of the emerging industrially and commercially based society of the Victorians, or, for that matter, the equivalent technological pressure of our contemporary society.

Much of this book has been, by implication, about the role of the teacher in the classroom. There remains the need to discuss the relationship of the teacher to other adults who may have a part to play in the classroom and the nature of the head teacher's role.

The untimetabled day, with its potential for increased choice by the children, soon reveals a wide range of interests. The older child interested in butterflies or rocks can be placed alongside an expert from the community (lists of secretaries and organizations, available at most public libraries are a useful source of contacts). Within the context of the workshop/studio classroom the extra adult does not cause a problem as would be the case within a formal classroom situation. In the same way children will be brought into contact with other members of staff (co-operative education rather than the meaningless but fashionable team teaching) with particular enthusiasms and skills. The flexible, fluid school organization not only makes such cross-references possible but actually encourages them. In this context we are talking about a community school rather than formal parent-teacher associations which draw on only a narrow section of the population. This is not to imply that this narrow section is not a valuable and needed group. The old-age pensioner sitting on the bench in the play area and talking about his own childhood has a contribution to the experience of six-year-olds as well as to the rising eleven-year-old carrying out some local historical investiga-tion. The pattern of work outlined demands closer links with the community at large as well as with parents of children in the school. Students on vacation (addresses are often available from local secondary schools or local education authorities) can be used as points of environment. The student with advanced biology can bring a richness of experience to a small group of children undertaking a pond study while an art student can be used in a print-making situation. The examples given are simple, but they serve to illustrate the nature of the opportunity open to us, while also indicating the vast progress still needed in this field.

The teacher in this context is seen as a leader taking a co-operative model of leadership in his work, involving children, outside adults and other teachers. The autocrat in charge of a teaching box or classroom is hardly adequate as a description. In this matrix the head must seek out his own role.

Just as the teacher derives his strength from his close relation-ship with children, so must the head advance the curriculum experience in similar terms. The staff meeting that becomes the case study conference is an example of the approach needed. The head cannot see himself in this situation or any other as the authoritative fount of all wisdom. One important role is the encouragement of areas of responsibility and opportunities of leadership for all members of staff. The head is a professional among equals, with certain extra areas of responsibility compared to ordinary members of staff. He has, of course, a particular responsibility for the process of change and growth of the school as a school and his awareness of changes on the wider scale will enable him to facilitate growth and change within his own school.

Perhaps the most depressing feature of our present situation is the isolation of one teacher from another, one school from another and the school from the community, both the lay community and the wider professional community of welfare, social and medical agencies. Communication must be a particular responsibility of the head. Just as the teacher puts one child alongside another to advance experience, or passes on an idea to another child, so the head begins by being the school gossip. His concern for human development ensures a selective approach to gossip! It is an historical fact that a large number of our primary heads have secured their promotion on the basis of a fairly simple pattern of class teaching where the class teacher was seen to be something of a rather talented actor-like personality with varying degrees of personal magnetism. From this background of experience so many heads seem to have developed an autocratic pattern of relationships.

As the pattern of teacher training and classroom work has changed so that we now demand a more complex and subtle response to the task of class teaching, so will the newly appointed head find it easier to see his role as head in a more complex way. The class teacher now sees his or her role as part consultant, part tutor, part instructor, part class teacher and part contributor to co-operative teaching within the larger unit of the school.

The head has the same wide-ranging pattern of work both within the individual teacher's classroom, working alongside the teacher, and in relation to transitory organized groups that run across the more permanent class or larger class cluster groupings. The head has a particular and further responsibility: he must respond selectively to the pressures from semi-official pressure groups concerned with curriculum change, parents, local education officials and indeed teachers within the school.

The role of the head is further discussed in the next chapter.

14

Heads and teachers

The Plowden Report* tells us that one-third of the children in our primary schools go to schools which are quite clearly good, while there are just over a hundred schools 'outstanding in their work, personal relationships and awareness of current thinking on children's educational needs'.

No one has analysed the situation which produces schools of such quality, though most teachers would be able to suggest the likely causes. It is a pity that we do not devote some of our research resources to a few small-scale studies of the causes of growth in quality in schools, rather than setting up curriculum mandarins to tell teachers what to teach. Observation indicates that the distribution of 'good' schools is not a random one nor are they distributed evenly throughout the country.

Superficial comments from some might lead one to assume that such schools depend upon the supply of brilliant heads, brilliant staff and brilliant children, but fortunately knowledge of the actual schools demonstrates that such crude sterotypes are quite misleading and do not reflect the reality of the situation. It is fortunate that ordinary heads with ordinary teachers and ordinary children can work together in such a way that their communities of children and adults become schools that are 'outstanding in their work and personal relationships'.

Perhaps the most important factor is the relationship between

* *Children and their Primary Schools:* A Report of the Central Advisory Council for Education (England) (HMSO 1967), paragraph 270

head and teacher and the head's interpretation of his role in the school.

'I am being paid to lead and I lead' is hardly an adequate perception of the task of the head. A full discussion of the task of the head is beyond the scope of this book, but let us briefly outline some illustrative examples. The head provides continuity of experience for the school and in most situations his appointment is of a longer duration than that of the majority of classroom teachers. This is certainly a responsibility that he should be conscious of, but it is not the most important consideration. A prime responsibility is to ensure that the staff crystallize their broad aims in the curriculum. The head will only be able to do this if he understands the nature of his relationship with his teachers.

In recent years the nature of relationships between father and child, mother and child, children within the family, between teacher and child in the classroom have, quite clearly, changed. Less widespread has been the acceptance of the need for a changing pattern of relationships between schools and the local educational authority and between the head and the teacher. The traditional head with his sense of isolation from the staff and an autocratic role in the organization and decision-making of the school has created a rich professional folklore and some obstacles to progress.

In contrast to the chain of command through the deputy head and the remoteness of the staff from decision making on syllabuses, ordering of stock and so on, we now have many schools where there is a genuine community of teachers fully involved in the affairs of the school. The process of change is highlighted in the examples of schools where the traditional head's room and desk has gone, to be replaced by a general meeting area with informal furniture for the use of all the staff, together with a number of smaller specialized areas for such secretarial and administrative tasks as the reproduction of information, letter-writing and so on, as well as a more private interview area designed to be an informal and relaxing situation for the use of head and staff in their meetings with parents and others.

Like all involved in the process of education, the head is concerned with the exercise of personal influence together with the stimulation and control of change. His success depends upon his sensitive understanding of the nature of personal relationships. Not everyone can come to know themselves, but most can discover the pointlessness of any leadership based on authoritarianism. If the head is to influence he must work with people and they must see him as one of the working community. A successful head realizes that he must use an approach in the school that is not unlike the approach of the sensitive teacher in the classroom.

The development of a creative and cooperative school ethos depends to a large extent on the efficiency of the use of permissive group discussions. It is in the group situation that aggressions and frustrations are reduced and it is in the isolated situation that they enlarge and become destructive forces. The staff working as a group have a common pursuit—the enlargement of their professional understanding of the developing school, with clear opportunities for responsibility and identification. Indeed, this concern can often be fruitfully extended from the group discussions of one school into a larger community of six to seven interacting schools formed into a 'parish', perhaps by an advisory teacher.

Of course, such groups can be viewed as cheap substitutes for individual psychoanalysis and, though there is a therapeutic element in such meetings, the use of group organization should not be considered in this way by the head or by anyone fresh from a year's lectures on 'Freud'! The situation is such that the mental health aspect is an oblique approach and the concern of the group is not with personal analysis or interpretation of motives but the consideration of practical professional problems that will involve everyone in practical activities. We are, in fact, concerned with how we exercise authority and the relationship between the authority of the head and the achievement of the other adults and children within the school.

Anderson's* study of dominative and integrative behaviour among teachers in kindergarten and primary classes showed that domination by teachers produced dominative and aggressive behaviour in children and that integrative behaviour by teachers produced co-operative behaviour among children. Lewin's experiments on dictatorial, laissez-faire and democratic leadership in teaching situations† are well known and provide supporting evidence for my plea to consider the role of the head in terms of democratic leadership. The point is so well accepted as tone of children due to the influence of studies in child development and so much more reluctantly accepted at the level of adult relationships that one is left anxious for the day when teachers no longer talk of 'child development' but talk and think in the context of 'human development'.

It is this basic understanding of the role of the head rather than concern with crude sociological discussions of the role of the head that is urgently required. Apart from the need to see the head's responsibilities within the groups made up by adults and children in the school, we need to remind ourselves of how best we come to understand. The duplicated syllabus, the lecture, the exhortation help little if at all.

Again the group discussion is vital, for the individual must be able to examine his feelings and insights within the group, bringing them into the open as he develops confidence. This process is shot through with the observations and experiences culled from the classroom and school situation and after a 'to-and-froing' period of this kind an intellectual understanding is reached. It is from this understanding of the nature of human relationships and the process of change that a head achieves a

---

* Anderson, H., 'Studies of teachers' classroom personalities', *Applied Psychology Monographs*, nos. 6, 8, 11 (1945–6)
† Lewin, K., *Resolving Social Conflicts* (Harper, New York, 1948)

position of influence and is able to respond to his responsibility to provide overall vision and leadership for the school.

Given this understanding of his role, what sort of opportunities face the head? The undoubted freedom of the English head brings with it possibilities of an almost unlimited nature. Unless he makes a selective response, a selective choice, he will fail to use his freedom. Indeed, there is depressing evidence that alongside the undoubted richness and quality within primary education there is a failure on the part of some to use their freedom.

The research of Joyce Morris* on the teaching of reading revealed that out of ninety classrooms there were:

Twenty classrooms without open bookshelves

Twenty-four classrooms with 'library books' in locked cup-boards

Twenty-four classrooms with no reference books.

Half the sample allowed the changing of library books to take place once a week.

Clearly the prime task for the head is to crystallize the broad aims in the curriculum, and the poverty of experience for the children in the classes described by Joyce Morris must be indicative of a failure of a sharing of any such vision between the head and the teachers concerned. It would be wrong to suggest that the sad state of affairs revealed by the Morris research is indicative of a deliberate refusal on the part of heads to accept the demands implicit in their appointment, but rather it is a lack of vision which is the result of isolation in the context of the school and the wider professional community.

Such isolation leads to a total failure to respond selectively to the administrative and curriculum pressures, and at its most destructive level we see heads making random interventions frequently related to warden-like control of circulation areas,

* Morris, J. M., *Standards and Progress in Reading* (NFER 1966)

litter and similar problems. The head has a choice of action and this is determined by his basic attitudes to people. Consider the following sequence:

10.15 AM Head arrives in the classroom of Mrs X on his morning check of classes before the 10.30 mid-morning break.

'Well, Mrs X, getting down to it, I hope. Eh! What's this? A finishing-off lesson in the morning?'

The teacher, despite the existence of a formal timetable, attempts to organize her own variation of an untimetabled day.

The head then moves across the room. 'What's wrong with you, lad? Counting your teeth for a graph? That's a new one on me. Going to be a dentist? No?' In an aside to the teacher: 'Just as well, with his brains', and then moves on.

'Ah, Barbara, where have you been? Going to the toilet at this time? Oh, you have been measuring your tree, have you? Did you ask your teacher whether you could go? No!' Aside to teacher: 'You must keep an eye on that one, Mrs X.

'This is the painting table, I see—these are the skivers, I suppose?

'Anita, nine threes?'

'Don't know.'

'Well you'd better go and find out and then finish your painting.'

10.21 AM Leaves for the next class.

This encounter between head and teacher and head and children is important. It builds up an experience of relationships in the school and conveys the vision (even if by default!) of the curriculum. We progress towards a primary school that gladly accepts the implications of our contemporary knowledge of the tremendous differences in the rate of development in individual children. We still need to learn more about children, but we do know enough to make arrangements for a range of individual differences in our teaching organization (even though there is still a need to become more aware of the special difficulties in the development of boys). The whole pattern of living and work in school is influenced by our knowledge of human development, and our concern for the emotional and social, as well as the intellectual, is in dramatic contrast to the intentions which underlay the elementary school with its emphasis on the three R's.

A brief discussion of some of the developments in the primary curriculum will indicate the progress made since the elementary school concept and illustrate the importance of a selective response to curriculum pressures on the part of the head.

Marion Richardson's* work is well known and it is an undoubted fact that she made a major contribution to the removal of a heavy overburden of adult-imposed subjects and the acceptance of a narrow range of work that could be seen to be conforming to uniform and imposed standards. The discussion of the work of Marion Richardson which follows is not intended to provide an adequate account of her influence but merely to highlight one aspect of the consequences of her work in many classrooms, far removed from her original influence both in time and, of course, personal contact.

To some extent the extended period of children's painting that followed the work of Viola, Cizek and Richardson could be seen in classroom terms to be a change of materials. Children were now to use large brushes and paint large pictures. To the extent that this was true we now see this type of work still undertaken and it clearly reveals the inadequacy of such an approach. In many schools the kind of painting associated with the Marion Richardson influence becomes dull and degraded as the child progresses through the school, and the teacher becomes remote from the whole process practised by the child.

It is the author's view that any curriculum change that merely concerns itself with materials in this way (and much of our present curriculum change in the field of mathematics, science and

* Richardson, M., *Art and the Child* (University of London Press 1948)

French is concerned with changing materials and content) has little value and is a source of imbalance in the work of teachers in schools.

In fact, the pioneering work of Marion Richardson in the field of children's painting became closely associated with another negative influence. The idea of the child 'unfolding' in his painting became imbued with psychoanalysis, and the interpretation of symbols and colours became the fashionable concern of many in education who were not (fortunately for the long-term implications) trained psychiatrists. The dual concern with materials as such and an external system of interpretation of symbols provided a quite inadequate framework for the teacher's action and evaluation and deprived him of the fundamental purpose of his work—working alongside the child in the process on which it was engaged.

The contrast between the consequences of the work of Marion Richardson within the field of painting and the pioneering work of Robin Tanner in the same field highlights the nature of the discussion required in any curriculum considered.

At first glance Robin Tanner may have seemed to be about the same business as Marion Richardson, changing the materials provided. Tanner's influence is recognized in crude terms through the provision of small brushes, pen and inks, pencils, watercolours and so on. But to discuss his contribution in these terms is misleading and such a framework for action would lead towards degraded work not involving the child, no better than that which now characterizes much of the 'Richardson' type of painting in junior schools. In fact, Tanner's work is concerned with a vision of the world, the child's process of seeing and sensual response to his environment. Art at the primary stage is an important means of discovering, revealing and recording the qualities of things. It is this process that is open to the influence of the teacher and it is this, together with an understanding of the scale of the child's world, that should enable a head to crystallize the curriculum approach for this school. It is, in the words

XXVIII

XXIX *Here the teacher has converted a cloakroom corridor into a set of working bays. This one provides a reading area. A table lamp, curtains, rug and other items make the most of what was a very unattractive and under-used area.*

of Laurie Lee, 'The three-foot high vision of the world, intimate, down to earth, sharp focus'* that the head needs to keep in mind. It is in this field of action that a selective response on his part will make a fundamental contribution to the pattern of work in the classroom and the experience of the children in his care.

With such a background to our consideration of the relationship between head and teachers we can usefully summarize some of the elements involved in his guidance of staff and development of the curriculum.

The head must accept the complexity of human development and not seek to develop a scheme for a timetable that is simple enough to hold in the mind but quite inadequate as a guide to action. He need not concern himself with timetables (any young teacher can be entrusted with the organization required to ensure that four teachers do not want to use the piano at once!), but he should be concerned with the arrangements of space, that is, the general differentiation of school areas to provide a range of opportunities and experience for children. This responsibility would include the organization of a large number of adults to provide points of contact for children needing an adult to listen to them reading, or for specialized advice on, say, bee-keeping or chess.

Using his influence within the group discussions, the head will be concerned to strengthen the observational basis of the work (both in the sense of using the environment and the observations of the professional teacher of children and the learning situations) so as to have available accurate observational descriptions of children to guide the work of the school. Again a selective response of this kind encourages a staff to restrict the negative curriculum pressures implicit in much of the packaged deal material from the semi-official curriculum renewal organizations. It is to be hoped that we are not about to return to the *Teacher's Weekly* type of curriculum experience when vast numbers of classrooms had similar displays of art or craft exercises.

* Lee, L., Talk on BBC *Woman's Hour*

The interventions of the head become concerned with the process of education rather than marking or testing. The head, like the class teacher, thus becomes involved in the recognition and nurture of growth points rather than the mere (and often misleading) checking of progress. The staff meeting becomes an extension of this way of working and the case study type of conference a more valuable influence on the development of a school than the traditional mixed bag of 'do's and don'ts' that make up so many staff meetings. In such a context there is a chance for the ordinary teacher to make an extraordinary contribution and for the head to claim that he 'hasn't any poor teachers'.

15

The school and the community

The urban downtown area is not just a pile of stones: it is a place where people live. In the primary school situation we know that the acceptance of the richness of any environment has a powerful consequence for our view of the curriculum and the opportunities given to children. The street with its shadows, textures, sounds, provides exciting starting-points for talk, painting, sketching, writing and mathematical investigations. Such an attitude and background experience should open our eyes to the human potential within any environment. As teachers we cannot afford to neglect the community and, apart from the obvious need to have additional adults within the school for a whole range of encounters with children, there is abundant evidence* that parents' attitudes (and this largely depends on the contacts with school) are vital in the educational process.

Regarding the curriculum and the general pattern of life within the primary school the Central Advisory Committee (Plowden) has done little more than gather together examples of good practice. In this respect it lacks the vision and sense of wholeness so powerfully expressed in the 1931 Report. But with its support for the idea of the community school it does provide a vision and a major undertaking for the next two decades.

* *Children and their Primary Schools:* A Report of the Central Advisory Council for Education (England) (HMSO 1967); Young, M., and McGeeney, P., *Learning Begins at Home* (Routledge 1968); Douglas, J. W. B., *The Home and the School* (MacGibbon 1964)

The Plowden Report defines community schools as follows:

> By this we mean a school which is open beyond the ordinary school hours for the use of children, their parents and, exceptionally, for other members of the community.*

The Committee give two reasons for making their plea for stronger relationships between parent and school:

> Parents have the right to know what goes on in their children's schools, and the right to any guidance they can be given about the support they can offer the school. The second and more important reason is the one implied by the results of the National Survey—by involving the parents, the children may be helped.†

We cannot afford to ignore the growth in positive attitudes of the parents of the children in our care towards the primary schools of their children, nor can we afford to neglect the richness of environmental resources within any area. We must also understand more fully the implications of sociological factors that lead to variations in family background. The patterns of working that stem from the untimetabled day make it possible (if not almost essential) to use a large number of adults in the day-to-day work of the school.

The minimum programme outlined by the Plowden report is probably generally accepted, but unfortunately not so generally put into practice. However, it is increasingly the practice to welcome every child and his parents when he is first admitted to school, or when he moves to a new school. Initial entry to infant

---

* *Children and their Primary Schools:* A Report of the Central Advisory Council for Education (England) (HMSO 1967), paragraph 121
† Paragraph 114

school is now frequently based on a staggered start with a small number of new entrants being admitted on each day, with the process spread out over several days. Preliminary visits are made by parents and child in the preceding term and thus the whole process is a gradual one. The preliminary visit of parent and child should enable the parent to meet the class teacher, see something of the work in the classroom as well as seeing the school under the guidance of the head. In addition to any open days parents should have an opportunity for regular private talks with the teacher. Included in the Committee's minimum programme is the provision for a school booklet, not unlike the prospectus of the independent school, and a general written report given at least once a year with an emphasis on general development and provision for comments from parents. There is also the need for some simple newsletter at various stages in the year.

Fortunately a proportion of our schools have a richer experience of community relationships than that outlined in the minimum programme, and our immediate task as a profession is to share their experience more widely.

Many years ago an infant school head drew up a list of resources within the area of her school. Each week members of staff visited their particular local contact to collect scrap card and paper from the printers, unsold papers from the newsagent, scraps of fabric from the tailors and dressmakers, and so on throughout the community. The head reserved the local undertakers as her personal contact and certainly the school has an unusual collection of scrap wood! One cannot disentangle contact of this kind, aimed at using untapped community resources, from the by-products of mutual contact and understanding, but it is clear that the prime purpose of our contact today is the involvement of parents because the children will be helped in a more fundamental psychological sense. However, the pattern of contacts with the community begun many decades ago by the infant head is still a valuable element in our work.

A group of parents making a pond and nature-study area for a school is an example of the creation of resources for the children that can lead to an understanding of the nature of the educational experience given to their own children in the primary school. The establishment of a workshop where parents can make bookshelves and mathematical apparatus is another example of the intermingling process, in which basic ideas can be understood through informal discussion and the strengthening of the material resources of the school. Most teachers can provide similar examples from their own experience.

The building up of an adventure playground is another example of parents working with the school, and it illustrates the responsibility of the teacher to guide the development of community projects while preserving the particular contribution of the school from the teaching point of view. The move to use the school plant for wider community purposes must not blind the teacher to the need to evaluate the impact on the basic purpose of the school of such secondary uses. The idea of using the actual school premises for an evening play-centre flies in the face of the needs of the children and the appropriate use of the school building. Converting the classroom to a play-centre for evening activities (and often these are little more than a range of games similar to snakes and ladders) fails to give the children a sufficiently changed environment from the ordinary school day, and the resultant problems of locking away school equipment and so on makes the ordinary daytime use of the rooms less efficient. At the end of a school day most children need the experience of an area similar to the adventure playgrounds already established in some areas. The building, too, needs to be more of a frontier cabin than a school.

The community school certainly needs to be much more of an open house to the area, but when we consider the facilities provided we need to utilize the complete site (adventure playgrounds, cabin for certain type of club activities and so on) as well as the actual school building.

In any new building programmes it is to be hoped that the idea of infant welfare rooms being attached to schools rather than church halls might be considered. Certainly, where space permits, the idea of the pre-school child coming into the school for an afternoon play-group session is worth considering. This is the time to begin the pattern of contacts with parents.

Evening lessons for parents, displays of work in local libraries and shops, educational notes in local newspapers and parish magazines are examples of the development of contacts between school and community. Links through letters to parents can ensure that some parents are able to watch television programmes taken by their children in school. Book lists of paperbacks can be linked with a special display in a local booksellers.

The examples already discussed illustrate the contacts that come from a view of positive use of the community by the school, but this is not an adequate response to the problem.

Education is not a process of doing things for people, or to people, but working with people. All parents and adults need to feel that they are accepted by the school and can work with the school. For every parent able to cover library books, repair furniture and do similar jobs there will be another parent able to contribute in a more direct way to the experiences of the children within the school. Most local libraries have a list of secretaries of local clubs and societies and within their ranks are a number of gifted enthusiasts who can share their enthusiasm and knowledge with small groups of children. The local secondary school will know of university students (particularly useful are the biologists and geologists) who may be able to give time during the year.

Alongside all these will be the adults who can listen to children talking and reading, or make an audience for a group anxious to share their discovery. On sunny days a garden seat in the garden area of the school can become the setting for two or three old age pensioners to sit and listen to young children and in turn to talk of days past. In this context we go some way to using the strength of the relationship between very young children and their grandparents. Of course, many of these retired people have skills of great value to the school. One school has a workshop for the making and repair of apparatus and this is under the control of a retired craftsman who gives a great deal of time to the work each week.

With the contemporary concern for the development of community schools we are confronted by the need to make choices without the advantage of very much background experience. We do not have the experience of American schools where teachers are accustomed to parents undertaking a wide range of tasks within the school.

One the one hand we have the rather shallow and meaningless pattern of school-parent contacts grafted on to a basically closed school community which, when combined with a teacher and subject-centred curriculum, serves only to create additional tension and conflict. It must be clear by now that there is very little scope for a parent in such a school or classroom setting.

On the other hand, there is the development of informal and far-reaching school-parent contacts where heads are in danger of assuming that they 'can do for' problem families what other social agencies have failed to do. In such circumstances the particular professional expertise of the teacher becomes misused and the nature of the experiences provided by the school diluted. Our concern with the family or community is because of our prior concern for the child, and we must recognize the multi-disciplined nature of any effective social action.

It is vital that the consequence of our concern with community schools should be the development of a much more integrated team approach by all social agencies. It would be a misuse of professional skills if all teachers were to be placed in the position where, because they were class teachers, it was thought essential that they should devote time to, for example, home visiting. And, of course, not every home needs visiting. Nor do we want to repeat the errors of the past made by some social agencies who took up the professional stance of telling parents about their mistakes in child rearing and care. Generalized and superficial advice from the 'outside' has no place in the developing community school. Generally we need to do much more *listening* to parents and very much less telling parents what to do. We need to think out very carefully our basic purpose in developing a community school.

Given that we have developed an untimetabled school with a range of individual and small group situations that throw into relief the need for more people within the primary school, we then have a natural point of entry for the community. On the whole the small scale involvement of people in tasks that they feel they can do will long remain the most important and obvious example of the community-school idea in practice. But, of course, no one would suggest that such contacts do not involve a deepening of psychological concern and understanding on the part of the parents engaged in the activities. The importance of parental attitudes in the development of young children is beyond dispute and the 'open school' idea ensures that both teachers and parents can share in this developmental process to a much more significant extent than before.

In the 'open school' children can still feel that home and school *are* different and that teachers and parents are different. It will not be a question of the teacher using his contacts with the parents to ensure that 'school' pursues the child to his fireside (or television set) in the shape of homework or of frequent assessment of the child through reported remarks such as 'teacher says you can do better'. The developing contacts will call for an increasing sensitivity on the part of both teachers and parents to the complex and subtle nature of the legitimate differences as well as the shared elements of home and school. In normal circumstances children have only one set of parents and the school must support and strengthen the special nature of this relationship, rather than making parents part-time teachers. In our concern for teacher supply let us not forget the basic importance of good mothers who know that society appreciates the vital role they play. It's a pity that the climate of our society is such that it can lead to the comment 'I am *only* a mother.'

The adequate involvement of the community in the school and the school in the community depends upon the adequate understanding, by the teacher, of what he or she should be about as a teacher. In such circumstances the contacts that come from the creation of an 'open school' can be seen as complementary and supporting, rather than as a threat to the teacher. Even so there are many new skills for the teacher to learn. The teacher has to extend the basic pattern of relationships within the school to include non-teaching adults while controlling their contribution to the total situation. A mother or another adult can listen to a child reading, can read to a group or take them to a near-by shop as well as helping with the preparation of materials, working alongside teachers and children. But tact will be required to ensure that they do not put brush to paint in order to 'improve' a child's painting nor can they be allowed to dominate a particular activity or room area by their constant presence. The teacher needs to know how to ensure that such adults become part of the ebb and flow of activity that makes up the primary school.

All this is a question of a developing sensitivity on the part of teachers which will come from discussions of common experiences.

Ideally the 'open school' should provide many different reasons for parents and others to feel that the school is a friendly and important place in their community experience. Group medical practice centres, infant clinics, libraries and old age pensioners' clubs—if they form a physical cluster of buildings—can form a focus for visiting and contact. But few schools will have this kind of facility, and then they must choose the kind of activity or activities they can allow to share their limited resources. Such choices must avoid the dangers of merely using the community rather than trying to become part of it.

We have already mentioned the importance of listening to parents and others rather than telling them what to do. A beginning can be made by giving time for the staff of a school to scrutinize the established pattern of contact with homes.

Let's look at the traditional report to parents. What do parents need? What have we expected to be the result of such comments as 'John needs to make more effort'? Might the parent feel that the teacher needs to make more effort? Does such a remark help the parents understand their child rather more? What does a second reading of the written reports reveal to the teacher? The two-way reports depend for their effectiveness upon the quality of the school section and we must be certain that our report format and comments provide a helpful context.

Let's look at the traditional (and rushed!) open-evening interviews with rows of supplicant parents attempting to preserve some semblance of privacy while the teacher takes up the stance of *telling* parents and calling them to account. Such meetings only serve to isolate home and school from each other. The informal but regular monthly meetings (the first Wednesday in every month) when parents know teachers will be about the school make for a more natural pattern of consultations that can be spread throughout the year. The joint working parties and other meetings all carry the opportunity for exchange of information and consultation.

In the open school home visiting can come about as a natural extension of a pattern of relationships or the more selective special approach to particular parents. It will still be a sensitive area and not all homes 'ought to be visited'. When a mother feels free to pop into a classroom and ask the class teacher 'Would Mr X [a student teacher at work in the school] like ham for tea because Mary has invited him to tea today?' a great deal of misunderstanding that comes from fear has been removed. Heads, and caretakers, school secretaries and teachers need to become very much aware of the fact that what is to them a familiar place can be a strange environment and source of strain. It is up to the school to convince parents that the school is open to them and that the community can contribute to the experience of children.

The pattern of relationships between school and community is good for the school in a limited curriculum sense and it is good because it allows the local community to identify with the school.

There is also the question of relationships with the professional community of managers, inspectors and near-by schools, the local authority and other organizations.

The success of the professional community is largely dependent upon the organizational pattern encouraged by the local authority. The role of the Advisory Teacher seems vital, for they can act as a focus for a group of schools, as school managers encouraging the particular skills of the heads in their parish. It is unfortunate that the suggestion that it is possible to reduce the number of H.M. Inspectors seems to be gaining widespread acceptance. Within the present structure of local-authority administration it is unreasonable to imagine that an enlarged body of local-authority inspectors would make an effective substitute for the Department's body of Inspectors. The very limited number of changes in the pattern of relationships between schools and local authorities is depressing evidence of the need for 'the office' to catch up with the changes in schools. Further, the very delicate balance between curriculum freedom and central influence is under very real threat from official and semi-official curriculum bodies. H.M. Inspectors have a proven and distinguished record within the curriculum field, of, at the lowest level, holding the ring for the pioneering teacher within the classroom and, at their best, encouraging the growth of ideas from the focus of all our activity—the classroom. There is no substitute for their influence, and any serious reduction in their numbers must be seen against the intense pressures in our contemporary society acting on teachers. The vacuum that would be left by a depleted body of Department Inspectors would soon be filled by influence of a more limited and sectional kind. Already there are indications that the reduction in the influence of the Inspectorate has resulted in unreasonable curriculum pressures being placed on some schools.

Teachers in schools are very much aware of the need for the

nature of the relationship between school and local authority and the various curriculum renewal projects to be carefully considered. Teachers need support in their daily task of developing a 'good school' and the importance of considering the development of children through the child's experience must be seen to be accepted as a framework for discussion and education. The social climate of a school and the emotional health of individuals needs the attention of advisers and others who are concerned with more than 'the parts' of a school. It would be a tragedy if lack of concern with the total experience of teachers and children was to have the consequence of inhibiting the slowly changing pattern of relationships now developing within the professional community, and the wide-open school or community school concept.

Index